REAL *Deal* ESTATE

NO SH*T SUCCESS TIPS
FOR REAL ESTATE AGENTS

PATRICK L. HANCOCK

Patrick L. Hancock -- 1st ed.
Chief Editor, Shannon Buritz

ISBN: 978-1-954757-35-6

The publisher has strived to be as accurate and complete as possible in the creation of this book.

This book is not intended for use as a legal, business, accounting, or financial advice source. All readers are advised to seek the services of competent professionals in the legal, business, accounting, and finance fields.

Like anything else in life, there are no guarantees of income or results in practical advice books. Readers are cautioned to rely on their own judgment about their individual circumstances to act accordingly.

While all attempts have been made to verify the information provided in this publication, the publisher assumes no responsibility for errors, omissions, or contrary interpretation of the subject matter herein. Any perceived slights of specific persons, peoples, or organizations are unintentional.

Dedicated to my wife Angie, my children Zach and Emily, who together continue to be my primary source of inspiration, my parents Pat and Sharon, and my brother Kevin. Words cannot express my appreciation for your love and support throughout the years.

CONTENTS

FOREWORD

The sleazy sales guy…we do everything in our power to avoid them. You know who I'm talking about. The car salesmen, timeshare salesmen (are these extinct yet?), and the kiosk salesmen at the mall just waiting to prey on the next tourist, spraying them with cheap perfume or showcasing their latest useless gizmos and gadgets. Before you can even speak, their exhausted and tired sales pitch is already in full gear. The stench of desperation surrounds the situation, and you're in pure dread. The adverse reputation of these salesmen precedes them. But somehow, recently, there's a newcomer to this hall of shame—the omnipresent REALTOR.

They're everywhere. There's likely one in your family, undoubtedly a distant aunt or uncle. If you're in a major city, turn your head left and right – then up and down. Not only did you achieve much-needed neck relief, but a realtor probably just crossed your sightline. Go ahead and post in your local Facebook group that you're looking to buy or offload a property. Crack open a cold one, sit back, and watch the vultures swoop in. Your post will be a deluge within ten minutes, guaranteed.

So, how do you separate yourself from the pack? What makes you different from the stampede of other realtors bursting through that door behind you? Surely, by this point, you have a robust marketing strategy, maybe a strong social media presence, and can throw in a couple

of good client referrals. You may have even sold a handful of homes during the historically strong market over the last couple of years. Unfortunately, what goes up must come down (at least partially). How do you pivot when inventory dries up, or climbing interest rates dissuade buyers and sellers? Is your success tied to the market's cyclical nature, or does it persevere regardless of its volatility?

Real estate is a results-driven industry, and Pat ensured we got results every time we threw our hat in the ring. To put it plainly, the tips in this book simply work. We couldn't have accomplished and scaled our portfolio without that separation factor from other realtor/investor duos. As an investor, if my REALTOR can source deals, run cash flow analytics, overview financing options, and charismatically negotiate, there's nothing left to do except give the final say. Gone are the days when a realtor would just serve as a client's liaison to the MLS, brainlessly shooting off listings that vaguely match their buyer's parameters. Newsflash: Your clients can download Zillow, Redfin, and Trulia to overtake this responsibility within their own time and convenience. The typical run-of-the-mill realtors have been devalued and sometimes even replaced by iBuyers (Opendoor, Offerpad, etc.). A great realtor makes themselves invaluable in all phases of the deal and does not just halt after the acquisition.

One thing is certain; I was lucky to meet Pat when I did. If that wasn't serendipitous enough, it happened at the brink of one of the greatest real estate runs in history in the scorching market of Central Florida. I was in my mid-twenties and just searching for my first home. After beating out an offer from Opendoor, I reached out to Pat again in six months after seeing the home's value skyrocket by

20% in a short period. What would happen if I had two of these houses? Three of these? FIVE of these? At the time, this was just wishful thinking. Little did I know that this first house would become a live-in flip and springboard our investing journey toward financial independence. Over the following years, we amassed a lean, seven-figure, multi-unit portfolio, ranging from single-family homes to condos and townhouses. We beat out properties with 10, 20, and sometimes 30+ offers in a blistering Orlando market. We learned creative ways to source off-market properties, unleashed our REALTOR, and the rest is history. I can rest easy, knowing with full confidence that my REALTOR is getting after it with my best interests at heart. While a typical investor might view this as a luxury, Real "Deal" Estate aims to make this the standard.

These days, while I attribute much of our continued success to the lessons learned in this book, I cannot understate the quality of the man behind its teachings. He is humble to a fault and religiously sharpens his sword with books, networking events, and any material he can get

a hold of. The hunger for improvement never fades. While I'm undoubtedly proud of our business achievements while working alongside Pat and partnering on countless transactions, I'm most grateful to consider him a close friend. I genuinely hope this collection of stories and teachable anecdotes through Pat's lens not only thrusts your trajectory as a realtor skyward but empowers you to be the best resource possible within your sphere of influence. Real "Deal" Estate will equip you to do just that.

Josh Parpia
Founder – HomeDUO LLC

WHY I WROTE
THIS BOOK

I have been in the real estate business in some capacity for seventeen years now. I have been a new agent, then a broker. I originally wanted to be the next Keller Williams and have hundreds of agents working for me—but that quickly changed once I got up to about 20 agents. I have purchased numerous properties for investment and owned a company similar to Rentals.com. I served as a mentor and coach to multiple agents over the years. I have experience in property management, commercial sales, residential sales, vacant land, and working with investors. You name it, and I have had experience with it.

During the past seventeen years, I have experienced many ups and downs. From unbelievably frustrating and downright depressing times to periods of extreme elation when those commission checks rolled in one after the other. Certain sections of this book will hopefully help you deal with these diametric opposite periods in your career. There is no more incredible feeling than depositing that check for $28,000, and there is no worse feeling than the stress of enduring long periods of zero sales. I have personally experienced both extremes.

When I first entered the business, my children were young, and due to my wife's schedule, I became the primary caregiver. I was the parent who dropped the kids off at school and picked them up, took them to their doctor appointments, and attended all the school activities. I was also the parent who took all the cars in for servicing and sat home all day waiting for service providers to come and fix something at the house. I was also coaching youth sports every day of the week.

At the time, I had obtained my broker's license and started my first real estate brokerage. Things were going wonderfully. I was hiring agents, had a couple of offices open, and even brought on a partner to help scale. Then, the stress hit. I grew up in a "Leave it to Beaver" household where we lived a modest life, and I do not think I ever stressed anything. Once my brokerage reached a certain point, the stress hit me like a locomotive traveling 100 miles per hour. The expenses kept piling on, and it seemed like sales were not keeping up. I also decided to be a "non-compete" broker, which meant I would not be out working with buyers and sellers and competing with my agents, and all my revenue would come from whatever splits I had with them. Well, that was a stupid decision.

Because of the stress, my blood pressure was off the charts. I was having panic attacks, anxiety-induced depression, and insomnia. The stress made me grind my teeth so much in my sleep that I cracked a molar! I started chewing my lip, too, which created a cyst that had to be surgically removed. I was a mess.

Most of you probably will not experience that degree of stress, but if you are an agent who needs to earn an income to help support the family, you will experience intense pressure at some point. It usually happens early on; if you just stick with it and work hard, it will pass. Whatever stress you feel, promise me you will acknowledge and address it sooner than later. Do not consider it a trivial matter. Trust me—I made the mistake of thinking that way, and my stress levels got so bad that I started hearing voices. I always was afraid to admit that I came close to having a nervous breakdown. After listening to an interview with Elon Musk where he admitted to almost having a nervous breakdown at some point, I thought, "Okay, if Elon almost had one, maybe it is okay to admit it."

I will categorically admit, with the utmost transparency possible, that not only have I experienced a significant amount of frustration and depression during my career, but I also have developed a resentment towards some aspects of the profession, which I address later in this book.

As an avid reader, I have read several books on how to become a top producer. The most famous one is Gary Keller's "Millionaire Real Estate Agent." If you have not read this book, then, well, I'm not sure what to tell you. Actually, I do know what to tell you—you probably do not read anything, and you're not going to make much money in this business. If I'm wrong, you can email me and let me know. I must also add that I am in no way advocating for Keller Williams over any other brokerage, as there are pros and cons associated with them all, but this is the first book you should read when you get your real estate license.

In addition to Gary Keller's book, there have been numerous other books written by top producers on how to be the best in the business, form a team, and more. However, most agents will never be top producers and do not have any desire to create a team. These books are all for providing warm fuzzies, which is great. As I said, Gary's book is one of the best I've read. However, I have not yet read a real estate book that not only provides you with what I refer to as "in the field" suggestions but also some of the many frustrations we encounter as agents.

Believe it or not, I absolutely and unequivocally do not care whether this book is a commercial success or if it makes me a million dollars and becomes a New York Times bestseller. I care that I accomplished my goal of writing and publishing a book, and I care whether or not you can take at least something from this book that will be of benefit. I spent about two years randomly jotting down notes and perhaps once every two weeks sitting at the computer to work on this. After reading several books on time management, habits, and execution, I learned just how important consistency is if you want to accomplish a goal. A "WIG," or wildly important goal. So, what action steps did I take? Instead of getting to the office, sitting down, and starting to work on answering emails and texts, I made it a point that the first thing I would do would be to work on this book. I probably wrote 2,000 words in two years, but when I made this small change and maintained consistency, I was up to 27,000 words in twelve weeks. Needless to say, it was a great lesson learned.

When researching how to write a book, the number one thing that stuck out was the recommendation to make sure to write about a topic you're passionate about. Given that I am obsessed with real estate and have been in the business for so long, it was a no-brainer that I would eventually write about it. As I previously mentioned, there are already hundreds of books written by top producers—the rainmakers of their huge teams who make millions of dollars a year. But I have never seen anything that addresses the "typical real estate agent." I decided that would be the direction I would take. I would address the typical agent since most agents work by themselves. To be clear, building a team is the way to dominate, but the reality is that most agents will never form a team, either by choice or by an inability to get it done.

I do, however, try to make suggestions and recommendations based on my years of experience that will hopefully help you in even the slightest way generate more business, enjoy it more, and handle certain situations better. I read this quote in "The War of Art" by Steven Pressfield and felt it was somewhat appropriate, "But the Muse had me. I had to do it. To my amazement, the book succeeded critically and commercially better than anything I'd ever done, and others since have been lucky too. Why? My best guess is this: I trusted what I wanted, not what I thought would work. I did what I myself thought was interesting and left its reception to the gods."

MY STORY

I was never an "A" student and was usually bored out of my mind in class. I spent much of my time doodling on the side of the paper I was supposed to be taking notes on. My most vivid doodling memories were of sketching individual football players, and each of my teachers was assigned a particular position. For example, Coach Humphrey was the quarterback, Mrs. Yates was the running back, and Mrs. Cardet was a WR—you get the picture. While I was not paying attention to my instructors and filling pages up with DaVinci-like sketches, I was always envisioning myself elsewhere, which always involved making money.

I started my first money-making venture when I was in middle school, and it was a neighborhood bicycle repair shop. I advertised, through word-of-mouth, that I was the local bike repair expert. Lo and behold—I found a few gullible friends that let me work on their bikes. I mostly worked on my own bikes, but I probably made about $50 in that first venture. Hey, $50 back in the early 1980s was big money for a 13-year-old.

My next business was more thought-out. I had always been interested in landscaping since my father often worked on something in the yard. A pond, a new row of banana trees, loropetalum, staghorn, philodendron, pineapples—you name it, my father planted it.

I usually helped. So my next big idea was that I would sell plants to the neighborhood. Since I had zero start-up capital and couldn't drive, I had a big problem to solve. Where would I get my inventory? How would I deliver the product? While I was out riding my three-wheeler (*remember those death traps our parents let us ride back in the day?*), I noticed that the area we rode in was covered in pine trees. Voila! I had my inventory.

I got up that next Saturday morning and headed out with my shovel to dig up my inventory. My father always had those black plastic pots that plants come in when you buy them, so I would dig up a small pine tree and plant it in one of those containers. I commandeered a red wagon from someone (*I still, to this day, have no idea where I found the red wagon*) and would walk house to house selling my pine trees. Genius, right? I'm sure you want to know how much money I made, and honestly, I can't recall, but it wasn't much. I know that my neighbor across the street bought three, and the last time I went back to visit my old neighborhood, those darn pine trees were still there. After 25 years, they were about 60' tall.

Once I started driving at the age of sixteen, I went and got a real job. Since I was in school and played sports, I only worked during the summers. But man, oh man, was it work. I dated a girl in high school whose family owned a large landscape company in Miami. Talk about back-breaking work. The good thing is that I was young and in shape, but damn, it was tough. I remember what was probably the worst day when we had to plant these tall palms in the middle of a highway. Well, the ground was nothing but rock, and we had to use a jackhammer all day long to loosen up the ground so we could get the shovels and scoop them up. I'll never forget when we put that first tree in, giving us just the smallest amount of shade. It was euphoric. It was also during that job that I had an allergic reaction to oyster plants. Still not sure if it was the actual plant or fertilizer on it.

In my last year in high school, and before I headed off to college, I started my own landscape business as I had learned a lot about plants and landscaping from my father and working for that company. This was also the first time I learned the value of reading. I started to purchase landscaping books and devoured them like crazy. I had a truck, a trailer, and even an employee when the job required. My employee was my buddy, Craig. I did not need him on every job, but when he did join me, it was always a blast. We had a tree trimming job where the trees extended over a canal. I didn't own any official tree trimming tools, so we climbed up in the trees and used our hand saws to cut off the branches. The branches were too large to fit in the trailer, so we just let them fall in the canal. We jumped and stood on all the branches piled in the canal to get them to sink. I know what you're thinking (idiots!), but we made $500!

It was obvious I was an entrepreneur from a young age, but the problem was I had never even heard the word *entrepreneur*. My parents were the furthest thing from entrepreneurs, and the school I attended was as strict Southern Baptist as they came. The only thing important to the powers that be was making sure you were saved and went to Sunday school. So my track in life was the usual—to graduate from high school, go to college, get a degree, and find a job. The problem was that I was interested in starting my own business, which I had already done several times.

Since I wanted to continue my lawn business, I started college intending to obtain a degree in Landscape Architecture. After two semesters of drafting and more math than I could handle, I said in my best Italian accent, *"Fa git about it."* Long story short, I have always had a passion for American military history and ended up with a degree in American History from the University of Florida. I had two options with that degree: teaching or attending law school. The latter wasn't happening, so I followed in my parent's footsteps and became a teacher. I taught middle school for almost eight years and met some of the most fantastic people. I'm still friends with many of my former students, which has been awesome. I quickly became burned out from teaching as it was just not in my DNA. The entire time I was teaching, and still to this day, one of my side hustles was selling military antiques. That was one way I could still run a business and perform my duties as a teacher. I cannot tell you how often I did deals at my desk. I guess that is why I always enjoyed film day!

When my wife and I had our second child, I decided it was time to make a change and get back to doing what I was meant to do. I started another business with a buddy whom I have known since we were kids. It was my first real estate-related venture and was an early version of Rentals.com. The business was called HomeRentalStore.com, and we advertised rental properties. At first, we were kicking ass. We were on the first page of Google, meeting with property managers regularly and trying to convince them we provided the best service imaginable, and things were looking extremely promising. The most encouraging aspect was that we were early in the game, and there were just a few other companies out there doing what we were doing. This was also before every real estate agent had their free brokerage-provided website.

Then, the dream was smashed. Google redid how they ranked sites; we plunged overnight from page 1 to page 55. A huge company whose name I can't remember anymore bought up and consolidated the larger companies, which caused us to look like a bass boat next to a cruise ship. The combination led to the utter destruction of the company, and in only a couple of years, we had closed our doors. But when you have tried and failed, that is when you learn the most powerful lessons. It took a few years of feeling sorry for myself to figure that out, but it is true. It was true then, and it is still true to this day. When I fail at something today, I almost get excited with the realization that I've learned something important and hopefully will never repeat it. If I did repeat it, that would be the classic definition of insanity, right?

When I was running the HomeRentalStore, I started purchasing my first investment properties. This turned out to be another early mistake. It was 2005-2006 when home prices skyrocketed, and every realtor I knew told me I needed to buy whatever I could find. If you're reading this book, please don't ever do that. Believe it or not, one of the realtors who encouraged me to do this ended up being my mentor. I know what you are thinking—trust me. However, in her defense, she was not a real estate investor. In hindsight, she wasn't an investor in any sense of the word. Rule number one in investing is to buy low and sell high. When I saw everyone running towards the real estate, I should have run the other way. But, as I said before, life lessons learned through failures are priceless. I will expound on this later, but in the investor world, true investors know not to work with real estate agents who don't invest themselves. When I look in markets outside of Florida, that is the number one question I ask. Do you own rental properties? By the way, BiggerPockets.com is the best source to find agents that are referred to as "investor friendly" and practice what they preach.

Over the past several years, my primary interest has been investing in real estate. I have also started working with more investors, but investing myself has become my passion. My first acquisition was back in 2005— I still have that one—and now, I manage a multimillion-dollar real estate fund with my good friend and partner. At the time of this writing, we have been in operation for just over a year and have 20 units in our portfolio.

01

DRESS FOR SUCCESS

I DECIDED TO START WITH THIS TOPIC FOR CHAPTER ONE. Not that it's incredibly important, but it's very timely for me. As I sit down to write this chapter, I have just returned from Parents Weekend up in Tallahassee visiting my son. Needless to say, it was another weekend of staying up too late, drinking too much beer, and overeating food. So here I am on Monday morning feeling like shit, exhausted, and my pants are too tight.

We have all heard the phrase "dress for success." It all starts with looking and feeling good. I don't want to offend anyone from the start, so I apologize in advance if I offend you, but honesty is sometimes painful. As David Goggins states in his best-selling book Can't Hurt Me, "if you look in the mirror and you're fat... you're fucking fat."

You need to get yourself in shape first and foremost. If you are not in shape, two things happen. First, your brain does not fire on all cylinders. You'll sit down at your desk (just like I'm doing right now) and daze in and out of that fog, and no matter how much coffee you try and slam down your throat, you will not have that laser focus.

Second, you need to work out so your clothes fit properly and you do not look sloppy. I have always been envious of those smaller skinny dudes that can wear anything tucked in and look like GQ models. My problem is I got into weightlifting and can eat like a horse. On top of that, I have no fashion sense whatsoever. Over the years, I became strong as an ox. Bench pressing 315 was my goal, and I achieved that at age 47. I had shoulder surgery as a result, but that is another story. I lift every morning for one hour and thirty minutes, and I am stronger than most guys in the gym, even those half my age. The problem is I'm 6'3", 240 pounds, and the bigger I get, the worse I look because I struggle with eating clean. I can look fat and sloppy in clothes, and it has always been a struggle for me. Hopefully, by the time you read this, I've trimmed down, and my pants fit right!

The point is—you need to take care of yourself to dress for success. Even if you're dead broke and just starting, look professional. I am a huge mindset guy, and as you read this book, you will notice I often reference that. Whether you work from home all day long or sit in an office, how you dress will help determine how much you get done. There is a proven difference in how much you can accomplish depending on what you wear.

Even if you work from home, you need to get up, put on some nice clothes, and pretend you are going to the office. Even if you do not leave the house the entire day, you will notice a difference mentally if you wear "work" clothes instead of sitting in your pajamas all day. Even at social gatherings, look nice. Over the years, I noticed that those individuals I considered successful looked nice wherever they went. Get into the habit of dressing well and looking professional wherever you go, as it is part of your "package" or overall presentation.

02

FAKE IT UNTIL YOU MAKE IT

*FF*ROM DAY ONE, YOU SHOULD ACT LIKE YOU ARE A TOP producer. Not only looking the part but acting the part. Dress like you make a million dollars a year and know everything about your market. Any opportunity to demonstrate that you're the expert—do it. Whether with a friend or on social media, act like you have been in the business for years. Anyone can dress for success, and anyone can learn.

I know there has been a trend over the past few years that does not agree with the "fake it until you make it" approach. I agree and disagree. While I will agree that agents should do things such as dress the part, for example, I do not agree with an agent pretending they know something that might put their buyer or seller at risk. An example I've seen for years is the real estate agent that says they work with investors but has no idea how to underwrite a deal. An experienced investor will catch something like that, but inexperienced investors will pay the price. I know from personal experience.

03

EXPERIENCE

HERE IS NOTHING MORE IMPORTANT THAN EXPERIENCE in the real estate business, and I'm not referring to the number of years you have had a license, as that doesn't mean squat. Having a real estate license does not mean you have experience. All it means is that you can receive a commission for real estate services rendered and that you passed the exam, which is not saying much.

Experience comes with your involvement in transactions, as every transaction is different. You are dealing with different people, goals, and problems that might arise. This is why you will hear me repeatedly stressing the importance of hiring a mentor or real estate coach with years of experience and involvement in hundreds of transactions. You need to realize whether or not you have enough experience to go it alone. If you average less than five real estate transactions annually, you need to seek out that mentor or coach to be there for you when something comes up, and believe me, something always comes up. As long as I've been in this business, I still encounter new issues that I've never experienced before. It is also important to note that it is okay to call someone for help. The greatest asset you have (that is, if you do not have a mentor or coach) is the legal hotline provided for free if you are a member of your Board. I would venture to guess that less than 5% of agents have ever called the legal hotline for guidance. I have and still call them when needed.

Remember, recognize who the experts are. You're not a legal expert; neither is your partner who you teamed up with because she's your buddy, and you want to call yourself a team. I have been involved with hundreds of transactions over the years, both on and off-market, while I was a non-compete broker assisting my agents and my own deals. These transactions range from residential, vacant land, commercial, and investment properties. I can still say to this day that every deal is different. Even if things go smoothly, you are still dealing with different personalities.

04

BUYING INVESTMENT REAL ESTATE THE RIGHT WAY

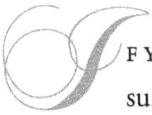

F YOU WORK WITH INVESTORS, YOU BETTER MAKE DAMN sure you know how to analyze investment property the right way. This is one of my huge pet peeves as I not only work with investors, but I am also an investor myself who owns numerous properties. I'll start by admitting that when I started working with investors and even when I first bought my own investment property, I had no idea what I was doing. I simply thought that as far as expenses go, you just needed to total up the mortgage, insurance, and property taxes and see if the rent you can collect covers that number.

Sadly most agents who work with investors still think that's it, and everything else regarding expenses can just be passed on to the tenant. Boy, oh boy, is that a big fat "NOT." Once again, if you work with investors or want to purchase an investment property for yourself, I encourage you to become a member of the BiggerPockets community. In the investor world, it is strongly recommended that investors only work with real estate agents that invest in real estate themselves. I think this is a wonderful suggestion, but unfortunately, like when it comes to selling any real estate, there are no criteria that agents must meet to show competence, only that they hold a valid active license. Please remember, when working with real estate investors, you need to factor in other numbers besides the mortgage, insurance, and property taxes. These numbers include projected maintenance costs, capital expenditures, and vacancy. BP has an excellent calculator to analyze rental properties on its website.

05

KEYS TO SUCCESS

HERE ARE SEVERAL KEYS TO SUCCESS. THESE ARE MY suggestions:

1. **Begin your day with your version of a "miracle morning."** There is an excellent book by Hal Elrod about this topic and plenty of information online. The best part is you can create something that works for you.

2. **Exercise and eat healthily.** I combined these two as they should go hand in hand. In my humble opinion, this is the most important as far as helping you reach your goals. If you are not healthy, eating well, and exercising, your energy levels suffer, and your brain is not firing on all cylinders.

3. **Dress for success.** This is tough for me as I have zero fashion sense and am a big guy. But keep working on it. They even have companies like Stitchfix and Stately that put together outfits for you and ship them to you in a freakin box! How cool is that?

4. **Be consistent with education.** This could be reading books, listening to podcasts, attending training opportunities, and participating in ZOOM sessions. I mean this in the friendliest and most gentle way possible, but if you are not constantly trying to improve through education, you will fall way behind those who do. When it comes to business books, my number one favorite topic pertains to mindset, and there are so many books today dealing with this subject, which in my opinion, is of the utmost importance. If you see yourself a certain way, you will act that way.

5. **Network.** You need to meet as many people as possible and form those relationships. I used to hesitate when using the phrase "it's who you know," but the reality is it is who you know.

6. **Have a personality.** I mention this in another section of this book, but if you are anti-social, have the personality of a fish, and do not consider yourself friendly, this is probably not the business for you. Be nice! Sounds simple right? Be friendly! Sounds even more straightforward. However, it takes work to always "be on," but you must do it. Eating healthily and exercising will help you maintain that feeling of positivity and keep you in good spirits.

06

QUALITIES YOU WANT
IN YOUR AGENT

THIS IS A CRITICAL SECTION HERE AS THIS FEEDBACK comes directly from the consumer. There are more, but the following appear to be the most common qualities consumers want to see in their agents.

- Trustworthy
- Experienced
- Responsive
- Gives maximum effort
- Knows the market

- Invests in real estate
- Has excellent communication
- Possesses negotiation skills
- Has good problem-solving skills
- Loves their job

07

IT'S WAY TOO EASY
TO GET A LICENSE IN
THE WILD WEST

N THIS BOOK, YOU WILL HEAR ME ALLUDE NUMEROUS times that getting a real estate license is way too easy. Every time I take a continuing education course (especially my initial licensure course), I feel like I have lost brain cells. The companies that offer the class courses make it extremely easy and tell you everything on the test, so you pass the test with ease (well, at least most people do) and want to continue to take their courses. I mean, if too many people failed, they would go elsewhere. When you sit and take the State test, you figure this out, which is why the pass rate is a mere 40% on the first attempt last time I heard.

Most agents find out pretty quickly upon entering the business that if they screw up, the broker has to deal with it, which is why brokers have to take out Errors and Omissions Insurance. What a crock. The agent screws up, and the broker gets sued. If that offends some of you, then perhaps you're one of those agents with a license because it is easy to get and keep. I am in no way, shape, or form one of the best agents out there. Countless agents sell more homes than I do (but I also don't "pad" my stats as many do and take full or partial credit for the deals that agents under me or part of my team procure) and are rock stars at selling homes. Some agents who are great at their jobs do not do a lot of business relative to some of the top producers out there. They are simply not as good at generating business.

But then there is that group of agents, and we have all worked with them at some point in time or sat next to them in class and said, "Holy Hell, how are they going to handle the buying or selling of what is usually someone's most significant asset?"

So what's the solution? I have always thought about that. Perhaps there is a minimum number of homes you must sell each year? I don't know the answer, but I doubt a change will ever occur. They did change the number of years you had to work as a sales agent before becoming a broker, but even that is a crock. I have a friend who just got her broker's license and opened up her own brokerage, and she calls me every two weeks with a question about how to handle this or that. I'm not talking about difficult or unique situations but about Real Estate 101-type stuff.

08

MANAGING
RELATIONSHIPS

ESIDENTIAL REAL ESTATE IS ALL ABOUT RELATION-
ships. If you want to succeed (and everyone has their
own definition of success), you must build relationships. In addition,
you have to add new connections to the mix constantly. That means
meeting more people through networking or any other method you
prefer.

I have found it extremely difficult over the years to add new
friendships and maintain those new ones and old ones. It has now
been seventeen years since I taught middle school, and I have lost
contact with probably ninety-nine percent of those individuals I
used to work with and had great relationships with many. I still

text, call or message many of them, but over the years, other agents have slipped in and created more solid relationships with these individuals. I will see a teacher I used to work with make a post on social media every few months that they just bought a new house. It would be someone I thought I still had a good relationship with. It was someone that was still part of my sphere and the database I consistently marketed to. However, I realized the genuine and honest relationship that used to be there was no longer there.

One of the difficult aspects of this business is not coming across as fake, such as only reaching out to someone for their business or referral. Now there is nothing wrong with that. Good agents who are top producers will not only build as many significant relationships as they can but also make those uncomfortable calls and ask their friends if they know anyone currently looking to buy or sell a house. I still struggle with it as I always have feared coming across as disingenuous. However, it is something you have to overcome. Create those relationships and maintain them as best you can.

My mentor never did a lick of marketing. She never spent a dime and looked at me as if I had three heads when I suggested that she start. She was killing it without the mailers, emails, databases, and social media posts. Her entire business revolved around creating and maintaining relationships. She went out to happy hours, played tennis, spent weekends at the ball fields, and volunteered at schools. She did whatever she could do to meet new people and create relationships, and it worked. She was also blonde, cute, had a great personality, and loved the social life, which did not hurt. If this is not you, you might need to use those mailers, emails, databases, and social media posts in addition to networking.

09

PERSONALITY MATTERS

INDING SUCCESS AS A REAL ESTATE AGENT WILL BE DIF-
ficult if you do not have a personality. How do you
know if you have the right personality for this business? Since it is
a relationship business, having zero personality will get you little
to no business. I had an agent like this. She had zero personality,
unfortunately, and averaged two sales a year at best, and these two
sales usually came from one friend she had that moved often and
invested in real estate. This agent did absolutely nothing to offset her
lack of personality. No social media, direct mail, nothing...nada...
zip...zero! I cannot tell you how often I met with her and suggested
what she could do to generate more business. Can you guess what
happened? She bounced from brokerage to brokerage, trying to find

that "right fit" and chasing the promise of a better opportunity, and she still sold nothing...nada...zip...zero.

Okay, she still averaged those two transactions per year through osmosis. I suppose that did pay for the family summer vacation, so who knows? Perhaps she was okay with only making $10K a year. Sounds harsh, right? I agree. However, I see agents that have been in the business for years that maybe sell a house or two a year, think they are full-time agents, but do nothing to add something new to the mix to help increase business. Why does it matter to me, you might ask? Every agent who is satisfied with just selling one to two homes a year to pay for the family vacation takes those transactions away from other professionals who do this full-time and depend on that income.

10

THE DANGEROUS AGENT

O NE OF THE MOST PUZZLING ASPECTS OF THE REAL ESTATE industry is the lack of quality control. I think most agents who have been around a while and are top producers will admit that there are a lot of bad agents out there. I cannot even begin to tell you how many agents do not know how to fill out a for-sale and purchase contract, much less know how to handle certain situations when they arise. Most have never used the Legal Hotline, and since most agents are only closing a handful of transactions per year (if that), they simply do not get the practice to become good at their craft. They don't attend classes, they don't read, and they don't see the value of having a mentor. I genuinely think the vast majority do not really need a job in the first place and are content with selling a couple of homes per year through osmosis and paying for that summer vacation.

The problem is that they make mistakes. Most never get caught, and if they did, who cares, right? The broker is the one who must deal with any lawsuit that might arise and hence has to carry Errors and Omissions insurance. This is why I stopped wanting to be the next Keller Williams or Re/MAX. I had hired approximately 20 agents and then realized I did not want to be a babysitter. I am more content with having a small team where I can hire the best and mitigate the risk of having agents screw up deals, leaving me on the hook. Now, don't go and get offended. I am not saying that all agents need babysitting, but a lot do!

11

GOAL SETTING

F YOU HAVE NOT READ THE BOOK *ATOMIC HABITS* BY James Clear, please do so as I consider it one of those "must reads," and it has been instrumental in making positive changes in my life.

Everyone sets goals, but the vast majority of those people never achieve those goals. To ensure you achieve your goals, implement the proper process that will allow you to do so. Immediately after reading *Atomic Habits,* read the *4 Disciplines of Execution.* This book is simply fantastic as well, as it pertains to actually how to achieve your goals. Whether you are an individual agent working alone or a top producer, this book will help you put the right process and systems in place using what is referred to as "Lead" and "Lag" measures to help achieve your "WIG" or Wildly Important Goal.

Let me give you an example. A few years ago, I became obsessed with lifting weights. It was part of my morning routine, where I would stop at LA Fitness on the way to my office. Talk about not having an excuse, as I passed right by it. Within the realm of lifting weights, my favorite exercise was the bench press. From the time I was in high school and started lifting weights (tiny weights, I might add), I had always wanted to bench press 315 pounds. If you do not lift weights and have absolutely no clue what the significance of the number 315 is, I will tell you. Most guys can bench press 135 pounds. That's a big 45-pound plate on each side of the bar (the bar weighs 45 pounds). The next "jump" is benching 225 pounds. That's two 45-pound plates on each side. The percentage of people in the gym who bench press 225 pounds is probably less than 15%. I have no actual data; this is just my observation. Now the next big jump is to 315! If you do the math, you will notice that each jump is about 100 pounds, which is no easy feat. I must also add that I was in my early forties when I started really enjoying lifting and making it part of my lifestyle and morning routine.

After establishing the habit of going each morning on the way to work and being consistent (notice those two keywords "habit" and "consistent"), I started to log what I was lifting each day, each week, each month, etc. Since the bench press was my favorite and the one I cared the most about AND had a goal, I placed a lot of attention to detail and focus on achieving my goal of bench pressing 315 pounds. Three hundred fifteen pounds is three 45-pound plates on each side of the bar, and I would venture to guess that less than 1% of the people who lift weights can bench press this amount. Put it this way: you notice when someone has 315 on the bar. I know some of you are saying to yourself, "Who gives a f*ck, meathead?" But stay with me here for a minute, as there is a point I'm trying to make. So, I would refine my routine week after week with my bench press. I would try resting a day or two days before to see what worked better. I would eat more or less different foods to see what made me feel stronger on the bench. After several months, I noticed I had an extremely specific and measurable (keyword: "measurable") formula. I even had my routine down to the minute by using my timer on the phone.

I had certain songs I would listen to as I increased weight and even had routines within the routines I would go through. After a set, I would stand up, turn my timer on, add the next amount of weight needed, sit back down, turn to my left, grab my towel, wipe my face, place the towel back on my gym bag, then turn to my right, grab my water bottle, take a sip, place it back down, wait for thirty seconds before the next lift, stand back up, check the weight to make sure it was correct, place my phone in my pocket, sit back down, lay down, then put the "right" song on and then came the lift. I would repeat it every time.

Now, as I'm sure you are exhausted by just reading that, you want to know if I reached my goal. Of course, or I wouldn't have used it as an example! So the point of this story is that I didn't realize it, but lifting 315 pounds was a "WIG" that I had. A WIG (Wildly Important Goal) is a goal you set for yourself to accomplish. Lead measures are steps you take to achieve that goal. Lag measures are the way you track or measure those steps. As previously mentioned, read the *4 Disciplines of Execution*.

It doesn't matter what field you're in, what you do for a living, or even if you work, we all have goals we want to accomplish, and this book will open your eyes to just why you have been so ineffective in achieving a lot of your goals over the years. Trust me, as this was my Achilles heel for years. I let the day rule me, and I had no control over my day. You know how it goes with this business. You have what everyone refers to as a flexible schedule, right? Well, the worst thing to do is look at your schedule as flexible. If you have that mindset, then you will be the one that has to pick up the laundry, take the kids to the doctor, go to the grocery store to pick up the three items that "we" forgot on Sunday, take the dog to the vet, stay at home and wait for the cable provider to come sometime between noon and 5 PM. Sound familiar? And while all this is happening, your phone is ringing, you are making calls, receiving and sending texts, and your head is spinning at a hundred miles per hour. It seems to everyone, including you, that you are getting a lot done, but you are not. Setting WIGs and using lead and lag measures will help you create routines that will develop habits, and the result is consistency, which is paramount in experiencing success in the real estate business.

12

THE CMA

S O NOW WE LIVE IN THE AGE OF WHAT I REFER TO AS ONLINE valuation models. Zillow, Realtor.com, Redfin, and NARRPR are just a few examples of websites and tools that provide agents with a supposedly market value of a home. Over the past several years, I have seen agents no longer take the time to put together a CMA (Comparative Market Analysis) and simply take the average of what these sites above provide as a value.

For example, let's say we have a house located at 435 Pine St., and Zillow provides a Zestimate of $450K, Realtor.com $470K, Redfin $462K, and NARRPR $435K. Too many agents are simply taking the average, which is, in this case, $454,250, and recommending to the seller that this is the home's market value. Since the vast majority of sellers automatically think you are an expert just by showing up, they believe you. The most accurate and professional method to arrive at a market value or suggested home selling price is to put together a CMA. The problem, however, is that most agents have zero clue how to do it. Here is me sounding like a broken record again - find or hire a mentor or real estate coach to teach you! Once that person teaches you how to do a CMA, you must practice until it becomes second nature.

13

SLOW DOWN

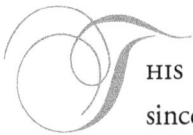

THIS IS PROBABLY THE BEST ADVICE I HAVE RECEIVED since I was in the real estate business. My mentor at the time, Tracy, noticed that every time I received an offer, I would call her frantically asking what I should do. Since I had just started in the business and nothing real-world is taught in your initial sales licensee course, I had plenty of questions. Sound familiar? Our process at the time was that if I received an offer, I would drive over to her house, and we would review the details. These were the days when agents still faxed each other contracts. So it was easier for me to just get in the car and drive to her house, especially since she lived about ten minutes from me. As soon as we sat down, the first thing out of her mouth was always, "Just slow down." She apparently could sense the combination of excitement and the "What the hell do I do?" bug eyes popping out of my head.

Years later, as I started my own brokerage and began hiring agents, I noticed that same excitement and the "What the hell do I do?" look from the newer or less experienced agents. Can you guess what the first words out of my mouth were? Yep, "Slooooooooww down," and I added, "Breathe." It sounds simple, but it really is excellent advice. Most agents do not do a lot of business, as I've said already, so when that offer comes in, they not only do not have the experience to handle it, but they are also so excited because I can guarantee the first thing they did was enter that commission number into the calculator!

Whether you're working with buyers making offers or sellers accepting offers, just slow down and breathe. You will make fewer mistakes that way, trust me. Not only will you make fewer mistakes, but you will also help prevent yourself from "eating crow." I'll be honest, I did this a few times early in my career, and I know that many of you reading this have done the same thing. You are working with either a buyer or seller and negotiating a deal when the other side verbally tells you that they have agreed to the terms in the contract. Because you get excited, your first instinct is to tell your client that "we have a deal," but you have absolutely nothing in writing. Then you find out that the other side changed their mind or the terms, and you have to go back to your client and break the bad news. Not only did you majorly disappoint your client, but you also made yourself look bad. Make sure you have it in writing before you make that call or send that text, no matter the situation.

14

FILL YOUR SCHEDULE

O VER THE YEARS, MY GREATEST CHALLENGE HAS BEEN STICK-ing to a consistent daily routine. Real estate agents have what everyone refers to as a flexible schedule. We can take the kids to doctor's appointments or run to the grocery store because we need Canola oil for dinner. Fuck that! I am telling you right now to fuck that mentality. If you do not create a consistent schedule and stick to it, you will, without a doubt, not be as productive. It all begins with your morning routine. Hal Elrod wrote a book called *The Miracle Morning*. I have not read the book yet, but many authors have incorporated Hal's miracle morning into their books so that I am constantly exposed to it in some form. There is also a plethora of information online regarding a miracle morning. There is no one perfect miracle morning for everyone. You can make your own based on what works for you, but the point is that your morning routine sets the tone for your day. My miracle morning consists of the following:

1. Wake up usually between 4:45-5 AM. Now, I will not sugarcoat this one. Waking up this early is tough. Especially because I suffer from sleep apnea, and there are nights when I just do not sleep well. One of my mentors (even though he does not know it and I've never met him) is Jocko Willink. Jocko (what an awesome name, right?) is a retired Navy Seal and was the commander of Task Force Bruiser during the Battle of Ramadi in Iraq in 2006. Jocko is now a bonafide entrepreneur. He's written books, has his own podcast, and tours the country, giving speeches on leadership. The guy is a true hero and inspiration. Perhaps his most impressive attribute is that he wakes up every day (I'm talking seven days a week) anywhere between 3:30 AM – 4:30 AM! To prove it, he takes a picture of his watch and posts it on his social media account. I used to wake up on average at about 5:45 AM, but adding that extra hour to my miracle morning has tremendously impacted my daily routine for the better. Jocko even has a ringtone that you can use as your morning alarm. I tell you what, having a Navy Seal tell you if you lie there in bed, you are weak and making a mistake is true motivation to get out from under those cozy sheets!!!

2. Head right to the bathroom (bathroom routine consists of peeing, brushing my teeth, splashing cold water on my face, and putting on my workout clothes).

3. Make coffee – Many of you reading this do not like coffee. I just absolutely love the taste and smell of coffee. I could

do without it, however. I do not rely on or need caffeine because, believe it or not, I feel the jolt of ice-cold water (that's number 4 on the list) more than I feel the caffeine. In fact, drinking that warm cup of coffee causes me to want to stay in my pajamas and get back into bed!

4. While the coffee is brewing, I drink a glass of cold water and take my vitamin supplements. Believe it or not, a glass of ice-cold water will wake you up, and it feels great.

5. Coffee is made, and I head to my chair to meditate. Yes, I said meditate. I just incorporated this one into the routine and still have yet to figure it out. Maybe if I write a follow-up to this book, I'll have figured it out by then. But hell, I'm trying! If you have not read the book *Breath*, I will encourage you to read it. I'm not going to get into much detail about it, but the book is about what the title suggests, breathing. In short, this is not doing the book any justice as it is an awesome and enlightening book, but breathing correctly is incredibly important. While meditating, you are supposed to breathe a certain way. This breathing technique is considered to help in many areas. But, as I said, I am still trying to figure this one out!

6. After meditating, I read. I used to despise reading. But just like anything else, it will become a habit if you do it consistently. I read seven days a week in the morning and usually go through about three books a month. I have come to look forward to it and really enjoy reading. I even get excited when that new book comes in the mail (I always order from Amazon). The most important thing I have discovered regarding the benefits of reading (aside from the obvious answer that you learn more about specific topics) is

that it allows you to see that third side of the coin. 99% of the population doesn't realize there is another side to a coin besides heads and tails. There is the edge! Operating on that edge allows you to see both sides of the coin (or both sides of the discussion, situation, argument, etc.), and seeing both sides of the coin enables you to be in more control of your emotions and not make emotional and irrational decisions. Perhaps that is the simplest solution to softening the tone on social media. People should read more instead of spending hours a day watching reality TV.

7. Eat a healthy breakfast – You are what you eat, and there is no doubt about that. Even if you work out seven days a week but eat like shit, you will probably look like shit too. Trust me, I know. I worked out 5 to 7 days a week and could bench press 315 pounds when I was 47. If you do not work out, that's damn good for a guy in his late 40s. I could lift a lot of weight and was strong. However, I ate like shit, drank too much beer, and had a sizable layer of fat over my muscles. The result was that I looked fat! Eating a healthy breakfast (you need approximately five to six smaller meals throughout the day) will jump-start your day with the right amount of energy to get you rolling towards success. I am not going to make suggestions as to what you should eat. It is not rocket science that eggs and oatmeal are better for you to eat than a McDonald's bacon, egg, and cheese biscuit.

8. Head to the gym – LA Fitness is on the way to my office, so how great is that? I work out for approximately 45 minutes, then shower and sometimes spend a few minutes in the sauna. Once again, I cannot stress the importance of

working out enough, and it is always best to get it done in the morning.

9. Head to the office, where I will arrive by 9:30 AM. Once I get to the office, I make another cup of hot coffee, sit at my desk and get to work.

It is essential to add that you must incorporate family time if you have one during your morning routine. Especially if you have children. As my kids' schedules changed, I've had to adjust my miracle morning over the years. This also means you need to put down your phone. Most of us in this business have been conditioned to the point where our cell phones are glued to our hands 24-7. It is not a good habit to develop when you are trying to carry on a conversation with your spouse or children while checking texts and emails. Put the phone down and focus on your family before and after work. Give them your undivided attention! After completion of my miracle morning, I head to work. Whether I arrive at 8:30 AM or 9:30 AM, my "deep work" begins promptly at 9:30 AM, where I time block certain tasks. I try my best to make my 9:30 AM to noon time sacred, where I am at my office every day. My current schedule looks like this:

9:30 AM – 10 AM: Work on writing my book

10 AM – 10:45 AM: Financials (this consists of both personal and business financials)

10:45 AM-Noon: Real Estate related projects

Noon to 12:15 PM: Make phone calls

12:15 PM – 1 PM: Lunch

After lunch is when I try to schedule appointments. As far as work relating to my real estate sales business, I'll try to get some done before the 9:30 AM time block begins or will take care of it after lunch. During these "deep work" periods, whether you are writing a book or lead-generating for your real estate business, make sure to eliminate distractions.

15

SEE THE VALUE

HIS SECTION MIGHT BE DIFFICULT FOR MANY OF YOU TO comprehend, as I have dealt with this so often over the years. Let me start by saying do not be cheap and learn to recognize value as an intangible asset. I will begin with an example. I had an agent who had never done a transaction involving vacant land. She had no idea there were vacant land-specific agreements, addendums, contracts, etc., and even less of a clue as to how to put a price on what the land was worth. As usual and as was typical, she wanted me to do everything for a few hundred dollars. I often met with her, helped her build a website, and joined her at listing presentations to help her get the listing, but in the end, I would usually lose money. The final straw was the vacant land deal.

She texted me that she needed my help, which generally meant a string of about nine texts in a row. I said I would be happy to partner with you on this deal and teach you how to run comps on land, complete the paperwork, etc., but not for a couple of hundred dollars. I even gave her examples of agents who had brought me in as a partner on specific deals because they lacked experience in that area. But this agent did not get it and never did. I told her the old saying, "Not only is my time worth a certain dollar amount, but also the value I bring to the table." Too many agents do not understand just how important it is to have a mentor, coach, or partner with whom they can learn skills and gain experience that will enable them to make 10x the amount of money down the road. Needless to say we did not work together on this deal.

16

LOOK THE PART AT LEAST

STOP DRESSING LIKE A SLOB! YOU WOULD BE AMAZED AT HOW many agents I see around town that look like they just rolled out of bed. Remember, as a real estate agent, you are always "on the clock." I promise you that you will bump into people you know at Publix, the mall, the ball field, the movies, and everywhere else you might venture out. I also promise you that you will see someone you know when you decide to dress down in your workout clothes during the day, as that has happened to me on numerous occasions. Now what is the problem with this, you might ask. The problem is, it's 11 a.m., and you look like you're at the gym. If you look like you are at the gym, you give the perception that you're not working or at least not working full time. People want to see agents who work full-time. I can say this from experience. It never fails that when I dress down and go out, I see someone I know, and it doesn't matter if I have just spent five consecutive hours working at my home office; it gives the impression that I'm not working and just came from the gym or I've been at home watching a movie, and that's a bad thing. You might disagree, but you should not be at the grocery store that often during the "work day" anyway. Or if you are, it should be on your way home from work or while you are out and about. It's a similar thought process described in Section 1 of this book. Dress the part as often as possible, or at least when you are "supposed to be working."

17

MOST AGENTS ARE CHEAP

F YOU HAVE NOT REALIZED IT BY NOW, CHANCES ARE (and I do not mean to offend you; I just want you to be aware if it applies) most agents are cheap, including you. You take every cent you make and spend it. Yes, you have to pay your taxes, but other than that, you blow your hard-earned dollars on a new iPhone, a family trip, and the twenty-seven items sitting in your Amazon cart. An exceedingly small percentage of agents set aside money for marketing. Then there is an even smaller percentage of agents who will send out a marketing piece after they receive their commission check, and that will be it until six months down the road when they receive another commission check. The most frequent routine I have seen is an agent selling a house in a neighborhood and then sending out a "Just Sold" postcard that claims they are the neighborhood expert and, poof, that's it. Remember, it is about TOMA (top-of-mind awareness) and consistency with your marketing. If you sell that house and send out that "Just Sold" card, follow it up monthly with another marketing piece, such as the neighborhood's market report. I might get a dozen different postcards from different agents in my neighborhood in a given year. But only one agent has done it consistently every month for years, and guess what? He dominates my immediate area. He also takes advantage of other opportunities, such as advertising at the local community movie theater during the previews. His office is right there, and he is always on the local social media group threads.

18

DIFFERENT BROKERAGE MODELS

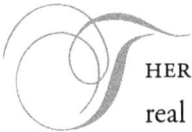

HERE ARE A DOZEN OR MORE BUSINESS MODELS FOR real estate brokerages today. Back in the old days, when there was just Century 21, Re/MAX, Coldwell Banker, and Keller Williams, it was the ole 50-50, 70-30, and 80-20 splits where you had to give them your left arm before you started making any money, especially if you were a new agent. Today you see everything from flat fee brokerage models where agents pay a fee per transaction or even a monthly fee. Any way you slice it, it's a numbers game, and you're just a number.

Every brokerage has a few "Top Producers." I had them as well. These are the agents who are great at what they do. They make the broker money, and the hundreds of transactions they generate over the years are fantastic advertising and branding for the brokerage. Whether they are individuals or part of a team, these agents genuinely matter to the broker. The rest of the agents are just a number; they come and go like the wind. The business model is that the more agents we can hire, regardless of quality, is the objective. Why do agents switch brokerages so often, and the broker never even knows? There is no rule that the broker must be informed, and real estate has to be the most transient of all businesses. Why is that? I'll address that later, but it usually comes down to the agent sucking and blaming the brokerage or that agent selling two homes per year and transferring their license to a brokerage that charges them $29 per transaction. I had an agent who, without going into too much detail, started with me and then left and came back three times. I think she had her license with six different brokerages in five years. At last check, she had not sold a house in thirteen months. So, I ask you, who is the problem?

19

EDUCATION, PLEASE!

I AM NOT SURE HOW TO SAY THIS WITHOUT OFFENDING some of you (as I am editing this manuscript, I notice that I say this often, but tough love is sometimes a good thing, right?) Still, the vast majority of agents put zero effort into education. They do not attend meetings, classes, or webinars. They especially do not read. This past year I read 35 books, listened to dozens of podcasts, and read several magazine articles, and guess what? You become better at your craft. Whatever field you are in, you need to educate yourself continuously. The first book any real estate agent should read is "The Millionaire Real Estate Agent" by Gary Keller. I started at Keller Williams, and they gave me that book. I've read it about five times since then. It is a fantastic book, and if you have not read it yet, you need to rethink your profession as it is the number one real estate book real estate agents need to read.

There are so many opportunities for agents to learn. The local board always offers free classes or very inexpensive classes. There are countless books on subjects related to the real estate industry or just business in general. Most agents know they are running their own business but have no clue what that means. Do you know the difference between a balance sheet and an income statement? If you are not used to reading or simply do not enjoy it, you will be surprised how easy it is to make reading a habit. When I added reading to my miracle morning routine, it was just a Monday through Friday thing. Not long after, it quickly became a seven-day-a-week thing. I would wake up on Saturday and Sunday and actually look forward to reading and feel like "I had to" before starting my day instead of watching those Abbott and Costello movies as I did on weekends for years. A great example of when you do something consistently for a while, it becomes a habit.

This is a very cut-and-dry topic. The more you learn, the better you will be, not just in your real estate business but in all areas of your life. You would be amazed that when you focus more on learning and less on watching reality TV, your brain craves more knowledge and less stupidity. I'll be honest; my wife and I watched A LOT of reality shows together. But thankfully, the more I started focusing on education, the less I could take of the non-stop screaming that seemed to embody the reality TV scene.

20

BE IN CONTROL OF
YOUR BUSINESS

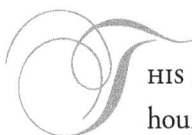

HIS IS TOUGH, AS THE REAL ESTATE BUSINESS IS A 24-hour, seven-day-a-week grind. Your friends, clients, and the complete stranger have absolutely zero conscience regarding your time. Some do, but most do not. Eighteen years later, I still get the phone call at 10:30 PM, the text message Sunday at 7:00 AM, or the "end of the world is coming" question on Thanksgiving Day. I highly recommend that you implement processes and systems that allow you to be in control of your day. One example would be to include in your voicemail that you return calls at a specific time during the day. That way, you are letting that person know when you will call them back and establishing the precedent by which you are on the phone. This business has the impression that you have to answer your phone whenever it rings. While there is truth to that, it doesn't necessarily mean you have to be the person who answers the phone all the time. Virtual assistants are a fantastic option for screening calls and taking messages. The more you can implement those processes and systems to help you take control of your business, the more production you will do, not to mention it will help prevent the stress and anxiety that can come from the constant bombardment of phone calls, emails, and texts.

21

KNOW YOUR NUMBERS

*O*KAY, I WILL BE HONEST HERE. I HAVE NEVER BEEN THE BEST at keeping track of numbers as I should. I am a right-brained visionary who sees the big picture and often gets lost in what my future real estate empire will look like while hanging out with Richard Branson kite surfing on one of his islands. But I cannot express the importance of this. If you cannot keep track of your numbers, hire someone who will. With services such as Upwork and Fiverr, you can employ bookkeepers for cheap. Knowing your numbers will allow you to see exactly how much money you are making and where your money is going.

Don't fall into the trap of starting to make money consistently, doing well, and setting up marketing, only to check your account two months later and realize you've spent 84% of your commission dollars on marketing. Even top-producing agents have issues with keeping track of their numbers. Can you guess the number one "number" that agents like to know but still, more often than not, most agents do not know? It is how much money they made the prior year. I have to file 1099s as a broker for my agents, so I track how much they make. The same goes for my assistant. It is comical that the agents and even those who make a lot of money often do not know how much money they made the prior year. It is understandable, however. Most agents, especially the good ones, are salespeople. That is what they are good at - selling. Usually, salespeople are not good at tracking numbers. It is essential to realize whether you are good at tracking your numbers. Whether it is simply how much money you made last year or how much you are spending on marketing, if you are not good in this area, hire someone who is. Virtual assistants are cheap! This was an area I had to improve in, and the only way I did it was to make it a habit of opening up my spreadsheet called "The Numbers" and reviewing it every day.

22

KNOW YOUR LISTINGS

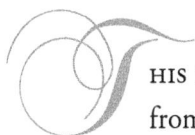

HIS IS ANOTHER ONE OF THOSE TEACHING MOMENTS from Real Estate 101 that still holds true and is one of the few things from class that still applies today. Not like back in high school when Mrs. Yates (my favorite teacher of all time, BTW) taught us how to diagram sentences. Knowing your listings is important. It never fails that when you have a listing, you will receive a call while you are sitting on the beach with a cocktail in hand, and you'll have to answer questions about the house. These calls usually come from passersby that see your sign and do not have the internet pulled up on their phone. I do not know why, but it happens. Maybe they think it is easier to bug you while you are on vacation. Now listen, if you have one or two listings, remembering the square feet, the number of bedrooms and bathrooms is manageable. However, if you have five, six, or ten listings, you either need to spend a few minutes reviewing your inventory daily or keep the MLS printout in your beach bag. Nothing will make you look more stupid and blow a potential sale than if a caller asks you to tell them about 123 Johnson Street, and your response is a big fat, "HUUUUUUUMMMMM."

23

THE THREE LS

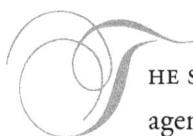

HE SINGLE MOST EXCELLENT BOOK FOR A REAL ESTATE agent to read upon entering the business is "The Millionaire Real Estate Agent" by Gary Keller. Yes, that is Gary Keller, who started Keller Williams. Now I am in no way, shape, or form recommending any brokerage over another. I will mention the differences between brokerages in another section of this book. But I will recommend books that you need to read. In a few other areas of this book, I have also said that you need to read, read, and read more. In "The Millionaire Real Estate Agent," Gary talks about "The Three Ls." The three Ls are Listings, Leads, and Leverage.

Let's start with the first two, which are the most obvious. As an agent, you should focus on getting listings. I know there are many agents out there who love working with buyers. I will never understand why. Not to mention it is not an intelligent way to operate your business. Listings generate leads or the second "L." Sales are all about leads. When you have a listing, you will receive inquiries from individuals looking to purchase a house.

The third "L" is leverage. This refers to leveraging your time by delegating some of your tasks and responsibilities to someone else. I am the most stubborn person on the planet when it comes to trying to do everything myself. In addition, let's face it, it costs money to hire people, so the natural thought is, "If I do it myself, I'll save money." Wrong! It wasn't until I read the book "Who Not How" by Dan Sullivan and Dr. Benjamin Hardy that I was finally convinced I had to delegate. I had tried before, but I am notorious for hiring the wrong people. A big part of the process is ensuring you ask the right questions during the interview and hire the right person for the job.

About sixteen months into the launch of my real estate investment firm, we were forced to pivot due to changes in the market. At first, I was sick to my stomach as things were going so wonderfully, and now we needed to make some changes. However, the change in the market caused us to make changes to our business plan. I had read "Who Not How" about twelve months prior and realized that now was the time I needed to focus on hiring some talented individuals to join our team. Within about six weeks, I hired a COO, a new bookkeeping firm, a content writer, and a new lead manager. Talk about an epiphany! It was the greatest thing since the birth of my children. Oh, my marriage and the chicken platter from Sonny's Barbeque topped that, but you get the point. Suddenly the speed at which we had been growing multiplied ten times.

24

MAGNET ON THE MINIVAN

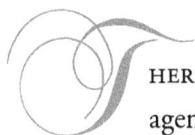

HERE HAS ALWAYS BEEN GREAT DEBATE ABOUT WHETHER agents should use a magnet on their cars. It is a personal choice and how much effect it has is probably extraordinarily small. But I must say, unless you drive a luxury car, DO NOT put a magnet on your vehicle. Especially if you drive a minivan that screams you are a stay-at-home mom (or dad) and do not work full time. You should also avoid placing a magnet on your car if you drive a beat-up 1999 Toyota Corolla with paint chipping. It just looks terrible, plain and simple.

25

PARTNERSHIPS

*L*ET ME BEGIN BY SAYING THAT PARTNERSHIPS ARE tough. They are just like marriages; if you are married, you know the ups and downs I am referring to. I have had several partnerships over the years, mostly involving real estate ventures but some involving businesses outside the industry. Most people partner with someone else for leverage. Whether to help with capital or a skill set you lack, very few business people or entrepreneurs who want to scale do it all by themselves.

Do not get me wrong. Partnerships can be incredible and help slingshot you to success and piles of money, but they can also go horribly wrong. First and foremost, you need to ask yourself whether you are someone who can work with a partner. For example, I have a friend who will not be happy unless he is the top dog barking commands. In any situation where he senses dominance over his position or whatever company or project he presides over, he feels threatened. You cannot have a partnership and feel threatened by your partner. Whether that pertains to you personally or your partner, you need to figure that out. Real estate is perhaps one of the more complex businesses to partner with someone.

As I mentioned, I have had partnerships in residential sales, real estate investment, and other non-related business ventures. Residential real estate has been the most difficult. In my experience, the challenge is determining who is responsible for what. For example, you and your partner decide to work together on a 50-50 partnership. One partner is constantly bringing in the business, and the other is not. The partner bringing in all the business must split the commission 50-50. This is the most common situation where real estate partnerships become jaded. I dealt with this situation when I started a brokerage with a partner.

Here is an excellent example of how a partnership can work to your advantage. My mentor, Tracy, and I were heading into a listing appointment. Tracy knew the seller and informed me she had recently gone through a difficult divorce. Her husband had cheated on her. Upon entering the home, I immediately noticed the seller had a cold demeanor, which only grew colder as we exchanged hellos and that typical small talk when you first meet someone. I am usually a friendly guy who, in my humble opinion, does well with first impressions. However, the feeling I got from her regarding her impression of me was, let me just say, less than stellar. It was so evident that she did not want to talk to me that I let Tracy proceed with the listing presentation, and I even remained in the kitchen during the walk-through portion of the meeting.

After the appointment was finished and we got back into the car, the conversation immediately turned to the apparent awkwardness consuming the air. Tracy told me that her friend was not too happy with men in general at the moment, given what had just happened with her former husband. Needless to say, I did not anticipate that going in, but I was extremely thankful I was there with Tracy, who could take over and save the day. We ended up getting the listing, and everything went just fine afterward.

Partnerships are also great when it comes to marketing. Direct mail, advertisements in magazines, etc., can be expensive. However, you can pool more capital with a partner to help with the costs. Complementing skill sets is another great reason to partner with someone. You will hear me say again and again that if you do not have a personality, it will be difficult to be successful in this business. If that's you, partner with someone who walks into a room and controls the crowd with the gift of gab.

26

BE VERY SELECTIVE
WITH YOUR BUYERS

*P*AY CAREFUL ATTENTION TO THIS SECTION BECAUSE, regardless of whether you are a new agent or one that has been around for twenty years, you will be confronted with BUYERS! We have all heard the saying, "Buyers are liars," and many are for sure. There are those slam dunk buyers who are usually friends or family, and when they call you, they are serious about not only purchasing a home but will, without a doubt, use you as their agent. Then you have those buyers who drag you around for months and disappear. The longest I worked with a buyer was approximately fifteen months. Now, this was not every weekend but on and off. However, this is a great story; I was just about to politely let them know that I was done and moving on when they called me up on a Friday night and said they wanted to see a house that next day. I showed them one more place, which was a great decision as they purchased that house. It was a sweet commission check as well. This is such a great example of things working out.

I also worked with an elderly couple on and off for about the same length of time. The difference was that they could barely qualify for a home, and their maximum price point was only about $115K. They had to have a single-family home in Orange County (Orlando). The problem was it was 2020, and prices were sky-high. We drove to Leesburg, Lakeland, Deland, Deltona, and other cities outside Orlando. It reached the point where I was done, but I felt bad and let my emotions get the best of me. I continued to work with them even after I realized that finding them a house they would like would not happen. The intelligent thing would have been politely letting them know I would have to move on. But I did not. Eventually, they sort of drifted out of the picture and, I believe, contacted another agent. I guess they could finally sense my frustration and dwindling enthusiasm.

27

SANDBAGGING

ACTUALLY MADE UP THIS TERM SORT OF. I'M NOT SURE why I used the word "sandbagging," but the practice reminds me of when I used to play and coach basketball. A good team who belonged in the A division would play in the B division to have a better chance of winning. If you read the definition of sandbagging in business, you will see that the term fits pretty well. How often have you represented a buyer and submitted an offer on a property? The listing agent immediately confirms receipt, and you have indicated that your offer expires the following day at, let us say, 5 PM. You selected the shorter time for a counteroffer or rejection because it is a seller's market and properties go quickly. The following day comes around, and it is nearly 5 PM. You have heard nothing from the listing agent, and suddenly that agent informs you that they have received multiple offers and asks for your client's highest and best bid. Typically, that listing agent could have spoken to the seller within hours of receipt of your initial offer but chose to talk to the seller and not get back to you or to hold off communicating with the seller until that next showing took place or another offer could come in. This is what I call "behind-the-scenes sandbagging." There is nothing wrong with it if the listing agent has not yet presented the offer to the seller. However, it can be highly frustrating for a buyer and the buyer's agent. Remember, there is typically no sense of urgency in a seller's market from the seller, but there is a sense of urgency on the buyer's part.

28

UPDATE YOUR E KEY

EFORE HEADING OUT TO SHOW A PROPERTY, ALWAYS remember to update your E Key. You do not want to show up at that first house and receive an error message because you forgot to update your key. It takes two seconds and should be part of your daily routine. I will never forget the first time I experienced this. It was a hot summer day in Orlando, and I was out showing homes to one of my very good friends. You would think that since she was a good friend, there would be no cause for panic, but when my key said "update" because I had not updated it, the sweat began to pour off my brow. I was already sweating because it was a hundred degrees outside, and I was wearing a long sleeve button down shirt, but this just made things worse. I also had no idea what to do because I was having connectivity issues, and the darn thing just would not update.

In addition, there have been times when I have received error messages. I have even had to call and ask customer service for help while my buyer was standing there staring at me with the "you are a dummy" look on their face. Sometimes it might take five minutes before your key connects with the box. Do not panic. Just let your buyer know that it is technology, and shit happens. Do not actually say, "shit happens," but come up with something witty, and all will be just fine.

29

ACT LIKE YOU HAVE
BEEN THERE BEFORE

CANNOT TELL YOU HOW OFTEN I HAVE BEEN OUT SHOW-
ing buyers a property, and my E Key gets an error code,
I cannot get into the combination box, or the gate code is wrong. It
is extremely easy to start sweating and panicking but do not. It happens to even the best agents, so remain calm and try to fix the issue.
If you cannot get your E Key to work, there is a number you can call.
If the combo to the lock box or the gate code is not working, there
is an agent number you can call. Over the years, it still amazes me
that agents use those stupid combination lock boxes. I understand if
the property is being rehabbed, and a general contractor must get in
and out. So there are times when a combination lockbox is needed.

However, in most cases, it is because the listing agent is too cheap to buy an electronic lockbox whenever I come across a combination lockbox. Agents, please spend the money and get an electronic lockbox. There are numerous reasons why they are better to use.

You will probably step in dog shit while walking around a property at some point. I did. There will be a time when you are trying to slip between the hedge and the side of the house to get to the iBox hanging from the hose bib, only to trip and fall into the bushes. I did. There will be a time when the enormous angry dog comes charging at you, and you let out a small scream. I did. Then there will be a time when you let the cat escape and have to go track it down. I had that happen. Oh yeah, and your GPS might take you to the wrong house because you entered the incorrect address, and your buyers are waiting for you at the correct place. It happened to me. I could go on and on. The moral of the story is to act like you've been there before!

30

WHAT TO BRING WHEN YOU TAKE BUYERS OUT

*I*F YOU ARE WORKING WITH BUYERS, ENSURE YOU BRING what I call "the essentials." The number one essential, believe it or not, is toilet paper. Yes, I know agents and buyers are not supposed to use the toilet in the house they are viewing, but you know as well as I do that 99% of you reading this have used the bathroom in a home you were viewing (or your buyer has!) Especially if you are considering new construction or recently built properties, most, if not all, will not have toilet paper. This goes for vacant homes as well. I honestly try not to use the bathroom at the home we are viewing, but sometimes the small bladder just can't hold off. I can't tell you how much money I've spent running to a gas station to use their restroom over the years because I did not want to use the homeowner's bathroom. Every time I used the gas station restroom, I felt compelled to buy something. But there were many times when I simply could not make it to the gas station. Make sure if you or your buyer has to use the restroom at a home, the water is turned on!!!

Other essentials to bring are a pen, paper, copies of the listings you will see, and water. If I was going to be out all day, I even brought small snacks. Typically, buyers do not want to stop and have a sit-down lunch, so having a small snack handy is a nice added touch. Not to mention, you will not have to sit there and listen to your or your buyer's stomach growling because they are starving.

31

DON'T BE POLARIZING

VERYONE KNOWS THAT THERE ARE TWO TOPICS YOU should not discuss with people: religion and politics. If you are in the sales business, and if you are a realtor, you are in sales, please refrain from not only discussing politics and religion but anything that could be considered controversial or polarizing. For example, I had an agent who just could not help himself when discussing his political views on Facebook. He was a staunch Democrat and felt compelled to blast the Republican Party and Donald Trump constantly. I had numerous conversations with him to no avail. I said, "Look, it doesn't matter what party you are affiliated with, but if you bash another party, you're going to lose 50% of your potential market of customers." The same holds true with other social media outlets.

One of my former agents lived in my neighborhood, and she would constantly post comments that made her look absolutely nuts. I had dozens of neighbors in the community make comments to me about how in the world I could let her work for me. So it not only made her look bad, but it was a poor reflection on me as well. 2020 was a year that made a lot of real estate agents look bad and lose business. If you were one of these polarizing agents who felt compelled to discuss politics daily on Facebook, do me a big favor. Go back and estimate how many minutes you spent engaging in politics on social media and equate that into hours spent. Now imagine if you had spent those hours on education.

Some will argue with me about my position on this, and I understand it, as I know some very polarizing agents. One is a top producer, and their comments and political viewpoints on social media apparently have no impact on their business whatsoever. I also know a dentist (yes, another profession) who is extremely partisan with their comments on social media but does more business than he can handle. So those who might disagree with me do have a point. They have told me that being polarizing or partisan might increase business. I guess it is possible, but it will depend on who your market is.

32

COMMISSION
CHECK FRENZY

AVE YOU EVER SEEN A SHARK FRENZY WHEN BLOODY BAIT IS
thrown into the water? The sharks go crazy and relentlessly
try to chomp on the bait. That is precisely how inexperienced agents
who make little or no money act when they sell a property and wait
for their commission check. I have had agents I have not heard from
in months come out of the woodwork and go into this frenzy when
they want their commission check. They text and call me more in
a day or two after closing than they have for months leading up to
that closing. These are usually the agents not interested in learning
anything or, as previously mentioned, will not, under any circumstances, read a book. It is usually the first check they've earned in

six months, and I tell you what, they make me feel like I had better get them that check before they starve.

I had one agent expecting her commission to text me for two days relentlessly. I was trying to watch a movie at the theater with my family when she began to give me a sob story about how she had three kids to feed, and I needed to get the check to her right then and now. I must add that she has a husband that works full time, and she works less than part-time as her real job is to take care of her three kids. But this is just an example of an agent losing their mind because they "smell" that commission check. My advice to you is to relax and act like a professional. You will get your check.

33

PAYING FOR THE FAMILY CRUISE

THERE ARE TWO TYPES OF AGENTS IN THIS BUSINESS. Those who work full time (really work full time and do not pretend to work full time) and those who get a license because it is easy and inexpensive, and if they can make $10K to $15K a year, they are satisfied. They are usually satisfied because they do not need to work but want to earn a little extra money to either feel like they are contributing or to, as I say, "pay for the family cruise." Whether it is a cruise or not, I'm referring to paying for the family vacation. I'm sure I will catch some flack for this, but do I care? No. I cannot tell you how many times I lost a deal to an agent who had no idea what they were doing.

They were simply better friends than the person who needed the house sold.

I have had agents over the years who had no idea how to fill out a For Sale and Purchase contract. One emailed me the offer package she was sending, which was absolutely butchered. I had to fill it out for her, and this was a $550K house where she would receive a $16,500 commission check. She showed her buyers two houses, spent a total of two hours with them, and had no clue what she was doing. If she did not know how to fill out the contract, do you think she negotiated the deal or looked at comps to get the best deal for her buyers? I doubt it.

I had another agent who was asked to list the house of a friend of her husband's. It was an elderly couple whose son had just committed suicide and were in a very distressed state of mind. My agent (I must add that she is no longer my agent, thank goodness) listed their late son's property well below market value, and it sold in one day. Not because she did such a fantastic job as their realtor marketing the home, but simply because she did not know how to look at comparable properties and underpriced the house during a hot seller's market with low inventory. She cost this poor couple potentially thousands of dollars because of her ineptness and greed.

A recent example involves my good friend. I even told him I would include this in my book, and since he's my friend, I can bust his balls. He called me up and said his sister-in-law wanted to buy a house. This guy has a full-time job and just keeps his real estate license active for shits and giggles. She wanted to purchase this $1.2 million house (3% commission being offered as a co-broke...do the math; that's $36K). He then asked me where he could find the "AS IS" contract. My pal hadn't sold a house in probably four years. Now he was representing a buyer in what was going to be the most significant purchase she's ever made, and he did not know how to find the contract to fill out and submit the offer.

So I've just given you three examples of transactions that always happen. Two things frustrate the hell out of me. The first is that we all know that the service being provided by these inexperienced agents is subpar and reflects on every agent in the industry. Secondly, that $36K should have gone to someone who works in this business full-time and invests the time and effort to provide quality service. They know what the hell they are doing. Perhaps the saddest part about these agents is that I can guarantee they cost their client money. This $1.2 million home was in another county, and I know my buddy had no idea what the actual value of this home was. His sister-in-law was paying cash and waived the appraisal contingency. Did she pay too much? Who knows?

34

CHOOSE A GOOD LENDER

*M*AN, THIS ONE IS HUGE, SO LISTEN UP. OVER THE years, I have used dozens of different banks and mortgage brokers. When I say used, I mean worked with, as my clients often use a bank or broker of their choosing. In this process, I have found a mortgage broker I practically beg my clients to use. She and her team not only know their shit, but their communication process is unmatched. Then, on the flip side, you have the "suck." By "suck," I mean these are the lenders that are just bad at their jobs. You have people who suck in every profession, right? Usually, it is not the banks but the independent mortgage brokers where you witness the "suck."

I worked on a deal once, and my client was a first-time homebuyer. My client did not listen when I begged her to use my lender and chose to use her friend's friend. It would have made too much sense to listen to me, right? The guy who has been in the business for eighteen years and has been involved in a shit ton of deals? So, we started the loan process, and the mortgage broker (let us call him Saul) dropped off the face of the Earth. About a week later, we hear from (let us call him Paul), who apparently works with Saul and is even less experienced. As days turn into weeks, we receive constant assurance that everything is moving along smoothly and my buyer will get loan approval at any moment. Now I must add that this was part of a four-house transaction.

The "Domino Effect," as I refer to it, is potentially complicated, but if all the agents and mortgage brokers/lenders know what they are doing, all should flow smoothly. So, we come to the closing week, and this clown informs us that we will need to extend the closing by at least another week. I will never forget the call because I was at my parents' house preparing to go fishing with my father. With four homes and families involved, moving trucks had already been scheduled, and all other moving preparations had been made. I knew this would quickly become a nightmare.

So back to the clown, and notice I have changed his name from Saul to "clown." During this week, he continued to assure us that my buyer would have her loan approval any day now and not to worry about anything. Well, I am sure you can see where this is going. After another week of pushing closing back, Clown informs us that my buyer will not obtain loan approval, and the house of cards comes crashing down. The moral of the story is, and again, my two cents: make sure you do your buyers a favor and try and convince them to use your mortgage broker that you know, through your own experience, is excellent at what they do! If you do not do a lot of business or are a new agent, remember it is okay to ask your mentor, coach, broker, or an experienced agent in your office who they recommend.

35

FIND A MENTOR

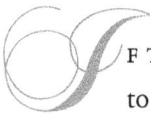

*I*F THERE IS ANYTHING IN THIS BOOK THAT I WANT YOU to do, it's finding a mentor. Whether you are brand new or have been in business for a few years, you need one. I cannot tell you how often I see agents float from brokerage to brokerage, thinking that this change will miraculously cause them to become successful and top producers overnight. If you are this agent, I have got news for you. The problem is you, not the brokerage. Remember, you hang your license with a broker. You are in charge of your own business. Those Real Estate 101 initial licensing classes you take are mostly bullshit. The school's business model is to make the classes so easy that all the students pass with flying colors, so they will come back and take continuing education classes there. It is a scam.

It always amazed me how easy it was to get a real estate license just by listening to many people in the class. Not to mention dealing with dozens of agents over the years who just plain suck and have no business in this business. In any business book, one of the commonalities you will hear is the importance of finding a mentor. It does not matter if you are a real estate agent or a wealth manager on Wall Street. Find someone experienced who has been doing what you are doing for a long time, and please remember that their time is valuable. You should also try and add value if possible. Since your mentor brings experience, perhaps you could volunteer to make phone calls for them? That is just one suggestion.

36

SELLING THROUGH OSMOSIS

I HAVE BEEN ASKED DOZENS OF TIMES, "SHOULD I GET MY real estate license?" People want to know how much money they can expect to make, which is always their number one question and concern. I always tell them they will sell at least 1 to 2 homes yearly through osmosis. If you are not familiar with the definition of osmosis, it is the process of gradual or unconscious assimilation of ideas, knowledge, etc. For example, "What she knows of the blue-blood set she learned not through birthright, not even through wealth, but through osmosis."

I could be completely wrong with my interpretation, but when I apply it to real estate, an agent is guaranteed to sell 1 to 2 houses annually with little or no effort whatsoever. If you have been in business for any length of time, you know what I am talking about. I am talking about the agents who do zero marketing, have no experience, and have the personalities of wet mops. Still, they sold that $450K home for a $13,500 commission check because their husband's friend felt he had to use them.

I had an agent once who was just plain awful. After ten years of being in the business, she had so little experience that she still could not fill out a basic real estate listing and sales documents without my help. However, she had a close friend who was a multi-millionaire and a real estate investor who used her as their agent. She would sell those 1 to 2 properties yearly because this friend felt obligated to use her.

37

YOU NEED TO LOVE THIS BUSINESS TO BE SUCCESSFUL

THE RESIDENTIAL REAL ESTATE BUSINESS IS A TOUGH one. There is a reason that agents make less on average than those in the garbage collection profession. It is simply too easy to get a license which means there are thousands of licensed agents, which then, in turn, means a heck of a lot of competition. You will hear me repeat this time and time again because it is true. In the business world, we talk about what is known as a "barrier to entry." Some industries or professions have a "high barrier to entry," meaning, for example, it might require a lot of capital to start or many years of learning a craft. An industry with little or no barrier to entry is easy to get into with little or no capital. Which one sounds like the residential real estate business?

At the last count, over sixteen thousand realtors were licensed with the local board in Central Florida. Yes, SIXTEEN THOUSAND!!! The result is a very high level of competition. Companies with a limited, low, or no barrier to entry usually experience this high level of competition. The truth is that all companies experience competition. Apple competes with Samsung with their smartphones. OfficeMax competes with Office Depot with regard to office supplies. However, imagine sixteen thousand OfficeMax and Office Depot stores in the city where you live. Imagine sixteen thousand Olive Garden and Bahama Breeze restaurants in your town. It is mind-blowing, isn't it? Loving your job will help you get to the top of the pile. Not loving your career as an agent will cause you to lose that desire for continued improvement.

38

SCRIPTS

HAVE NEVER BEEN A FAN OF SCRIPTS. LET ME BE CLEAR, though. Not being a fan of scripts does not mean scripts do not work. One of the most successful real estate agents I know is a master of using scripts. He was the agent who talked me into obtaining my real estate license. His son was friends with my son in preschool, and I will never forget being at a birthday party for one of the kids, where he used a script on me to demonstrate how effective they were. It was like Luke Skywalker using a Jedi mind trick on those Stormtroopers in Star Wars. Even knowing what he was trying to convince me of, he still managed to convince me. It was absolute Jedi shit right there.

Even after the demonstration and becoming a believer, I have never used a script in the real estate business. Who knows, perhaps I would be more successful if I did. My humble opinion is that scripts are for some but not for everyone. I do however, now have my virtual assistants use scripts when they make phone calls for my investment company. Yeah, I know it doesn't make much sense, does it? Just call me slow to the party.

39

STRUCTURE YOUR DAY

E ALL STRUGGLE WITH THIS ONE. WE ARE REAL ESTATE agents and have been taught from day one that you better always have your phone glued to your ear. I cannot tell you the number of times I have been out with friends, and if I did not answer the phone, they would make some smart-ass comments. It was always something like, "Don't real estate agents always answer the phone when it rings?" In fact, my partner always mentions that "Mark" (a commercial broker who is a mutual friend) is always on his phone. Whatever dude!

You need to answer the phone, but not as often as you think. If you learn about proper time management, reducing stress, structuring your day effectively, etc., you will see that the most successful individuals block off certain times of their day to answer and make phone calls. If you do not, I can promise you will never use your day effectively and limit yourself to what you might accomplish. You might be saying this sounds extreme, but I can assure you it is not. Put the phone down and block off time when you can check texts and make calls. Some agents do it first thing when they get to the office and right before leaving it. Other agents will do it during their lunchtime. Some do it 4 to 5 times per day.

My observations are that most agents are engaged with their phones constantly throughout the day and never get any "deep work" done. There are also serious health implications resulting from not allowing yourself to disconnect from your business. I can honestly say that after being in the real estate industry for eighteen years, I still haven't found a way to disconnect from work altogether. I think that is a combination of just how my entrepreneur's brain works and the nature of the business. Real estate is truly a 24-7 job. I think the only day of the year when I have not been called, texted, or emailed regarding real estate has been December 25th. Not that I do not expect it. However, it makes it difficult to disconnect truly.

I'll close this chapter with what I guess you could call a funny story. My phone constantly rings throughout the day, often driving me crazy. One day I received 63 phone calls, believe it or not. Those days are not typical, but between the texts and the phone calls, by the end of the day, my stomach was in a knot, and when I heard that phone ring, it made me want to cringe. To solve that problem, I chose one of my favorite songs as a ringtone (Paradise City by Guns N' Roses). Not only are they one of my favorite bands, but their guitarist, Slash, is my favorite guitarist of all time. I thought, "Now, when the phone rings, I'll hear the song play, and it will make me happy instead of feeling sick to my stomach." Well, that backfired, and now whenever I hear that song on the radio, it makes me cringe. Fortunately, they have a dozen other songs I love!

40

REDUCING YOUR
COMMISSION TO GET
THE DEAL DONE

*N*ow I know you have to be very careful when discussing commissions, and if you did not know that, please take the time to educate yourself regarding the discussion of commissions. Antitrust laws prohibit agents and brokerages from discussing commissions in certain situations. For this section, I am simply addressing the decisions you have to make as an agent regarding your commission. Depending on your brokerage, some agents have greater flexibility in adjusting their commission. Agents have attempted to charge a certain percentage for decades, but that has changed over the past few years due to different business models inserting themselves into the industry. Examples of these would be online buying platforms like Zillow and OpenDoor and brokerages that advertise flat fees. Agents tend to refer to the latter groups as "discount brokerages." Regardless of what brokerage you hang your license with, you have to make the business decision that is best for you and your client regarding what you charge for commission. Don't listen to the agents that chirp and chirp only to charge a certain percentage that had been considered "standard" for years. Do what works best for you and your client to get the deal done!

41

KEEP A CHAIR IN YOUR CAR FOR INSPECTIONS

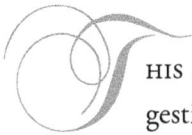

THIS IS A SHORT SECTION BECAUSE IT IS A GENIUS SUG-gestion and does not require much explanation. Keep a folding chair in your car for inspections. Many homes are vacant, and having a chair to sit on during that two-hour inspection is just plain brilliant, especially if you are an old guy like me with three prior knee surgeries!

42

REMEMBER YOU ARE THE EXPERT

YOU, AS AN AGENT, FROM TIME TO TIME, ARE GOING TO WORK with a client who has a strong personality and thinks they know everything. While your initial reaction might be to back off and perhaps be afraid to correct them professionally or provide a suggestion, you have to be the expert in the room. That's why they hired you, and that's what you have prepared for.

43

HORROR STORIES

WE ALL HAVE THEM, AND WHILE MOST ARE USUALLY NOT
our fault, we could have avoided many through experience.

- The buyer's agent represents the buyer in purchasing a
custom-built $900K home in a high-end part of Orlando,
Florida. During the inspection, it was noted that the water
heater was not working properly. The seller agreed to replace
the water heater. During the final walk-through before closing, the buyer's agent and the buyer walked the house and
did the typical inspection to ensure the house was as it was
during the initial inspection, checking to make sure appli-
ances were still working, there were no holes in the walls
from moving, all doors were working, maybe turning on a

few water sources to make sure water was coming out, etc. If you are like me, you will check to ensure the hot water works. This buyer's agent did that but only checked a few of the water sources, unaware that all of them were on the same side of this two-story house. After the buyer closed and moved into the home, the buyer realized that the hot water was not working on one side of the house, the side opposite the water heater. Long story short, the builder plumbed the house incorrectly. The house was only two years old, and the previous owner, the builder, certainly must have known there was an issue, which is why the water heater was replaced. The buyer had to hire a plumber to replumb the entire house, which required cutting approximately twenty-five holes in the wall, which then needed painting. Needless to say, it was a complete and expensive mess. The previous owners agreed to pay for half of the cost, which is an admission of guilt to me. In hindsight, the buyer's agent should have tested the hot water in all house areas, especially given that the water heater was newly added. Believe it or not, most agents do not check for hot water. If they turn a water source on, it is usually to check for a leak. So the lesson learned, regardless of whether or not the inspection noted a possible issue with the water heater, is checking all water sources for proper flow and hot water. The greater lesson learned is always to take your time and conduct a thorough final walk-through.

- A listing agent representing a seller on a home finds out after closing that the house was infested with termites that the seller had covered up. The seller was elderly, and her son flew down from up north to help her do some repairs on the home before selling it. While working in the kitchen, the son discovered extensive damage to the rear of the cabinets from termites. The son proceeded to make new back sections for the cabinets and nailed them over the damaged pieces. When the new buyer moved in, they had a newer refrigerator that could not fit underneath the attached cabinets. The buyer proceeded to remove the cabinets only to find termite damage. As they were now suspicious, they continued to remove parts of the cabinets, only to find more damage. There were even termite tracks underneath the wallpaper throughout the entire kitchen. A few weeks later, the listing agent began receiving photos of the damage from the buyer's agent, and it was an "Oh shit" moment! The listing agent drove down to the house to inspect it in person; sure enough, it was more than obvious what had transpired. After threatening legal action, the seller agreed to pay for the damage and new cabinets. The seller denied knowing anything about it, and the son was nowhere to be found.

- A listing agent represents a seller of a home built in the 1930s. The seller had previously had an electrician come out and attempt to hide the fact that aluminum wiring still existed behind the walls. Inspection results indicated that aluminum wiring did exist. Several thousand dollars later, the seller had to replace the aluminum.

- An investor purchases a high-end condo and does the walk-through the day before closing. This is why I like to walk through as close to closing as possible. The investor walks in the front door and hears a dripping sound coming from across the unit. The AC handler was across the room, and the investor assumed that was the source of the dripping sound. However, as the investor walked closer and closer, he realized the leaking sound was coming from a bedroom. Upon entering the bedroom, the investor noticed the ceiling had caved in, and water was pouring out onto the carpet. It was a top-floor unit, and the fire sprinkler had developed a leak. The good thing was that the association took care of all the repairs since it was "outside" the drywall.

- This is an example of why buying at the height of the market can be extremely risky. That old saying, "When everyone is buying, you need to sell," and vice versa. In 2005, an investor I knew was desperate to purchase his first rental property. This was when inventory was low, and properties would be on the market for days and receive multiple offers. This investor fell into the trap and paid $197K for a three-bedroom, two-bath condo. After the market crashed, his condo dropped to $70K! Seventeen years later, the condo peaked at $165K. Sure, he now has equity in the property but loses money each year because he has no room for maintenance, vacancy, and capital expenditure costs. The lesson learned is that agents should advise their clients that if they buy at the height of the market, this same thing could happen. The more you know about investing in real estate the right way, the more you will learn that there are ways to purchase investment properties that will help hedge against market crashes.

- Please do not take the seller's word about how old the roof is. The buyer's agent represents a buyer on the purchase of a $400K home, and when the seller was questioned as to the age of the roof, the seller responded that it was a "newer" roof. In my mind, "newer" means anywhere from 3 to 5 years old, but that is not always accurate. The buyer purchased the house and came to find out down the road that the roof was ten years old. There is a big difference, especially in Florida, where thirty-year shingles only last about twenty because of the intense sun and heat. Not to mention insurance companies today do not like to issue insurance on roofs over fifteen years of age. Agents must realize that they can search for permits online to confirm when the roof was installed. If you cannot locate the permit, use caution and factor that into your offer. The inspector will be able to shed some light on the roof's condition, but remember that inspectors are not roofers. If you cannot find the permit, one option is to have a licensed roofing company come out and inspect the roof. However, the issue is that most roofers will suggest you need a brand-new roof. But the point is, do as much due diligence as possible to determine the roof's actual age and do not take the seller's word for it.

- The "domino effect" (which I discuss in another section of this book) can have significant implications if something goes wrong. The buyer's agent represents the buyer in the purchase of a new home. The buyer's agent also represents the seller of that same home, who was attempting to purchase a new home for themselves. The seller of their new home was in the process of also buying a new home, and, on top of that, the seller of that home was moving. In case you lost me there, four families and four houses are all in the equation. The first buyer who started this "domino effect" failed to obtain financing. This was due to Covid, and her hours at work were decreased, so it messed up her monthly DTI (debt to income ratio). This is not uncommon, but the news that she would not obtain financing came so late that the wheels were already in motion; one family had already moved out, another family had all their belongings sitting in a storage pod in the driveway, and another family had all their belongings in boxes in their garage. It was a complete mess and very disappointing for all those involved. This "domino effect," whether it is with two homes or more, is common. However, the more properties involved, the greater the challenge. I would highly recommend that if you are in a transaction where there are multiple properties, and you have little experience, you get help.

44

INVESTORS CAN SPOT OTHER INVESTORS

*D*O NOT BE OFFENDED BY A LOW OFFER. AN OLD SAYING goes, "If you are not embarrassed by your offer, then it was too high." The straightforward interpretation: Do not be afraid to make a low offer, as you might get a better deal. You have probably seen this more with investors submitting offers on properties. Typically, you list a property, then suddenly receive an offer via email from an investor who hasn't even seen the property. The offer amount is usually well below the asking price.

For example, I had a condo listed for $120K. Within twenty-four hours, I received an offer via email for $88K. The investor never saw the place but knows that if he purchases the property for $88K or even $95K, he has acquired the property at a great price where his numbers would work. Being an investor myself, I not only understand what is happening, but I also do that. Unfortunately, when this happens, the listing agent often presents the offer to the seller in a negative light, and the seller gets offended. Explain to your seller that this is an investor, and they must purchase the property for a certain amount.

45

REMEMBER YOU ARE DEALING WITH MOSTLY EMOTIONAL INDIVIDUALS WHO CAN OFTEN MAKE IRRATIONAL DECISIONS

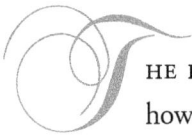

HE PRIMARY IRRATIONAL DECISION OFTEN CONCERNS how much the seller thinks their house is worth (owner pride). If I had a dollar for every time a homeowner told me their home was worth more than it was, I would be able to buy that Vail mountain cabin I've had my eye on for several years now. Owner pride is something that all agents have to deal with. Make sure you have done your research and can show them why their house is worth what it is worth. If you use Zillow's Zestimate instead of the CMA to try and take the easy route, you will often have difficulty justifying the value you come up with, and it is just the lazy way to go.

Emotions are also challenging to deal with when presenting feedback to sellers. Let's face it; some houses look like shit. They often have strange odors and can even pose a danger by just walking through them (I slammed my head into an awning so hard it almost knocked me out as it was hanging too low due to a broken hinge, and another time almost went through the floor because it had rotted out). Be honest with the seller no matter how uncomfortable it is because if you don't and the house sits on the market for a long time, that seller will blame you and hire someone else. Do yourself a favor. If the seller has six dogs and two ferrets and you can barely breathe because your allergies are on red alert, let the seller know. It is difficult, I must admit, to be honest about feedback such as, "The house looks like shit," especially when it really does look like shit. In this scenario, you have to get creative in what you say to the seller. In other words, be gentle.

46

BE CAREFUL

SMALL MESS OR REPAIR MAY BECOME MUCH MORE SIG-
nificant and costlier. This happens quite frequently. The
inspection report comes back, and the buyer sends a list of what
they would like repaired. Negotiations occur between the seller and
buyer, creating a list. The seller then hires the appropriate service
provider to take care of the repairs, and everything is peachy keen,
right? Well, not always.

I had an instance where I was selling a historic home built in
the 1920s. The inspection report noted an old knob and tube wire
running up through the attic. If you aren't familiar with knob and
tube wiring, it was the type of wiring used back in the day for elec-
tricity. The seller agreed to have the knob and tube removed as it
was supposedly a dead line that served no function. However, when

the electrician came out to replace what was thought to be a dead wire, half the power was lost when he cut it. Long story short, it was an active wire that ran through the entire house. What should have been an inexpensive repair turned out to be an extremely costly one, as the seller had to replace the whole wiring system. The moral of the story is before your seller agrees to fix any repairs that could be costly, get an estimate first.

47

ADDENDUMS

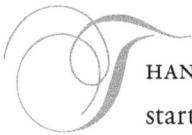

HANKFULLY, I TOOK THIS GREAT CLASS BACK WHEN I started at Keller Williams, taught by an agent named Yien Yao, and it was all about the For Sale and Purchase Contract. Yien explained how agents making alterations or additions to the contract could easily subject themselves to liability and do an injustice to their clients. Remember, this is a legal document drafted by attorneys, and any change you make sticks. Most agents do not change what is already written but will add terms under the Additional Remarks section. Some agents would tell you to have an attorney help with this, but unfortunately, that is not practical. Be very, very careful when adding terms to the Additional Remarks section. I have seen many agents make mistakes or insert unclear and vague remarks. Perhaps the most common mistake I have seen pertains to seller contributions to the buyer's closing costs. Below are some examples that could mean entirely different things depending on the wording.

- Seller concession to the buyer of 3%
- Seller credit of 3%
- Seller will contribute 3% toward the buyer's closing costs
- Seller will contribute 3% of the purchase price toward the buyer's closing costs
- Seller will contribute up to 3% of the purchase price toward the buyer's closing costs

48

SHARPEN YOUR AX

HARPEN YOUR AX, ESPECIALLY DURING PERIODS OF DOWN-
time. Most agents, especially early in their careers, will
experience long stretches of downtime. There are always going to
be periods of downtime in this business. And by downtime, I am
referring to instances where you might not sell a house for several weeks or months. The old 80-20 rule (also known as Pareto's
Principle) applies, where 20% of the real estate agents do 80% of
the business, so the other 80% of agents can often experience long
periods between deals. During these periods, you must maintain
focus, which is why having a scheduled routine is so important.
Real estate is becoming increasingly competitive, and agents are
reducing their commissions more frequently, which means most
agents are making less money.

At the time of this writing, there are over sixteen thousand realtors in my market and only 5,859 homes available for sale. Do the math on that one! The combination of low inventory and lower commissions means that more and more agents are doing less business and making less money. Maintain your routine and continue to sharpen your ax. There is no shortage of educational materials or opportunities to meet more people to add to your database. You can even look for other options as a side hustle to make more money. Ideally, your side hustle would be something that relates to real estate.

49

DO NOT EXPRESS YOUR FRUSTRATION WITH THE BUSINESS

*O*KAY, HONESTY TIME HERE. THERE HAVE BEEN TIMES WHEN I was so frustrated by this business that when someone asked me how real estate was going, I would say something to the effect that it sucks. No matter your career, there will always be rough times. Especially if you own your own business, the path is a winding one. When I opened my first brokerage early in my career, I was cranky, stressed, and a tightly-wound ball of grumpiness. I had several offices, a bunch of agents, and two small kids at home. I was also a "non-compete" broker, where I would not participate in buying and selling homes with clients.

Simply put, I would not compete against my agents. As the overhead grew, babysitting agents increased, and my children's schedules became busier, I grew even grumpier. I still remember one of my good friends, Karen, coming up to me in the parking lot where our kids attended the same school and asking me how real estate was going. I told her I hated it and could not wait to get out (that was probably sixteen years ago, so needless to say, I have since had a change of heart!) No matter how you feel about your business, never say something like that. Always remain positive and give the impression that you love your job and are doing great through the good and bad times.

50

DON'T CONDUCT BUSINESS WHILE DRINKING

KNOW IT SOUNDS SEXY, AND YOU SEE HUNDREDS OF PHO-
tos on social media where the sharp-dressed guy or gal
is drinking scotch or sipping a glass of wine and making a business
call from their 125' yacht. If it is a guy, he probably also has a cigar
hanging from his mouth and a scantily clad young lady in an exceedingly tiny bikini sitting behind him in a lounge chair.

Suppose you can keep to a single scotch or a single glass of wine
that does not affect you, then fine. But if you enjoy drinking beer
like I used to, you must be incredibly careful. Remember, you are
in the real estate business, where you are expected to answer that

phone whenever it rings or respond to that email when dealing with something time-sensitive.

I cannot tell you how many times I was on vacation, it was Saturday at 5 PM, and after being out in the sun all day drinking cold beer, a client or agent would call me about something without fail. It's not that I was a blistering drunk who couldn't hold an intelligent conversation. If concerned that I would sound intoxicated, I would not answer the phone and let it go to voicemail. But there were plenty of times I answered the phone, and I am sure I sounded a little too chatty or giddy as a happy drinker. However, every so often, if I encountered one of those agents that just rubbed me the wrong way, my ability to maintain my patience went out the window as I can also have a noticeably short fuse. So, keep the drinking under control whether you are on vacation and need to talk on the phone or out to dinner with clients or potential clients. Not to mention too much alcohol consumption is a bad thing all the way around. It affects your health, your sleep, and your brain.

51

THE LAW OF "THREE"

VERYONE KNOWS THREE AGENTS. TRY THIS. THINK OF all your friends, and then think of how many real estate agents they are friends with. I can guarantee that each of your friends knows at least two other agents. I will never forget the first time I started to notice this. Early on in my career, I was sitting at my son's baseball practice with four other individual parents. I am outgoing by nature, and given that I was also trying to let them all know I was in the real estate business, I started a conversation with the guy sitting next to me. Since the bleachers we were sitting in were small, the other parents were within earshot of our conversation, and the next thing I knew, we were all talking. After about thirty minutes, it turned out that three of the four of us were real estate agents. That was also the first time I realized that there are too many agents out there! At my good friend's 50th birthday party this past weekend, I was sitting at a table with four other realtors! It's sort of humorous on the one hand but on the other, gheesh! I'd recommend the "less is more" approach in those situations. Too often in that setting, the competition starts to set in for who is the best agent at the table, and it never fails that the agents who engage in this type of behavior end up looking silly.

52

INVEST IN A QUALITY
PHOTOGRAPHER

T HAS BEEN AMAZING TO SEE HOW MANY AGENTS HAVE used their iPhones to take photographs of their listings over the years. Not to mention when a dog or cat is part of that poor-quality photo. Drones have become a large part of photo-taking these days. Even though they are cool and can take excellent aerial shots, drones are not always good if the surrounding homes are covered in blue tarps and have fallen fences and debris littered around the yards. Hire someone good and pay for it. Remember, 99% of potential buyers start their search online by looking at pictures.

53

LOOK FOR ANGLES,
NOT ANGELS

*W*HEN YOU HAVE A LISTING THAT IS NOT SELLING, IT'S not always due to the price. Usually, it is, but there are ways you can add value to the property by providing other uses. I had a listing once that was an older house that needed a lot of work. It was sitting on a large lot and in a great location. The usual process for most would be to list this property on the MLS under the residential section. However, after doing my due diligence and having experience on the investing side, I discovered that the lot could be subdivided and two homes could be built. The numbers didn't work for either demolishing or renovating the original house, but the numbers did work if the lot was subdivided. So look for a possible angle vs. the angel to swoop in and buy the house in the traditional fashion.

54

KNOW YOUR "CAP X"

*W*HETHER YOU ARE WORKING WITH A BUYER, SELLER, OR investor, obtain a complete picture of your Cap X. What does "Cap X" mean? Cap X is an abbreviation for Capital Expenditures, which refers to the big-ticket and more expensive items such as the roof, the HVAC, the plumbing, and the electrical in the home. Regardless of who you represent, know the status of these items, especially in an older home.

For example, homes built in the 1960s used galvanized steel for plumbing. Galvanized steel has a life expectancy of approximately 50 years, so if you purchased a home in 2020, don't you think it's essential to find out if the plumbing has been updated? Even then, that's not good enough. The plumbing might have been updated in the 1990s when builders used polybutylene piping. Both galvanized steel and polybutylene are prone to leaking.

Understand the difference between the different types of roof shingles and their lifespan. What do you do if you find knob and tube or aluminum wiring? It's not only a good idea to have a basic understanding of these higher-cost items but also how much it would cost to replace something if needed sooner or later.

55

DON'T BE AFRAID
TO NEGOTIATE

*M*ANY AGENTS JUST WANT TO SAY YES AND PUSH THE
deal along, afraid of any perceived risk that might
threaten the deal. The first thing to do is realize who has the leverage. In a seller's market, automatically, the seller has leverage. Add in a buyer who can only afford a house up to $220K. In my market, these homes go like hotcakes. Primary occupants and investors scarf these up as soon as they hit the market. This only provides the seller with even more leverage.

Regardless of the market, be bold and negotiate on behalf of your client. Chris Voss wrote a tremendous book on this topic called "Never Split the Difference." How often have you said or had someone say to you when trying to agree on a number, "Let's just split the difference?" It feels like everyone wins, doesn't it? Unfortunately, that's not always the case.

56

SHOWING FEEDBACK

KNOW I'LL CATCH SOME FLAK FOR MY OPINION ON TAKING time out of my schedule to provide showing feedback to a listing agent. While I understand it's a nice and thoughtful thing to do and is considered by many in the business to be a common courtesy, does Winn Dixie take time to give Publix constructive criticism? Does Elon Musk take time from his schedule to call up his competition and "help them out?" Maybe he does, but I doubt it. Once again, I know it sounds harsh, but I'd rather focus my time and energy on my business. Between the businesses I run, publishing a book, and spending time with friends and family, little time is left to sit down and let a listing agent know what my buyer thought about their listing. I'm sorry, but my time could be better spent somewhere else.

57

TOMA

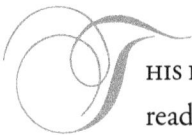

HIS IS ONE OF THOSE THINGS THAT, WHETHER YOU HAVE read a business or real estate-related book, you should know about. It is one of the basic concepts in any business. TOMA stands for "Top of Mind Awareness." It is a fundamental and straightforward concept that will impact your business perhaps more than anything else you do. TOMA means just what it sounds like; being the first name that pops into someone's head when they think "real estate agent."

99% of agents who advertise do it so inconsistently that it becomes a waste of time, money, and energy. An agent will sell a house and send out "Just Sold" cards. An agent will list a home and send out "Just Listed" cards. An agent will send a market report to a neighborhood twice a year. Good start, but it just does not work. In real estate, we use the term "touch." Yeah, I know it sounds creepy, but you must "touch" people (your sphere of influence first and foremost) consistently.

There is plenty of data online and in books that will tell you just how many times you need to touch someone, but the point is that it has to be consistent. Remember, everyone has at least three friends that are realtors. I used to say everyone knows three realtors, but since there are so many licensed agents out there, everyone has three friends who have a real estate license. Stay top of mind, and on top of that, look like the expert. Whether you like it or not, you compete with those friends for business daily.

I have found over the years that a combination of marketing strategies works best. The most important and effective one is relationship-building with your sphere of influence or those closest to you, such as your friends and family. Take them out to dinner. Attend social gatherings. Call and text them on the phone. In addition, send out bi-weekly emails and monthly direct mail pieces. No matter what you do, you want it to look professional but believe it or not, so few agents do a good job of consistent marketing that anything you do is better than nothing.

And please do not forget to follow up after a transaction is complete. I've seen too many agents represent a buyer or seller on a deal only to not follow up for years, expecting the client to call them when they are ready to buy or sell again. What happens is that during those years of no contact, your client has met another person who has become a friend, and they have a real estate license. Guess who is top of mind now?

58

YOUR SPHERE OF INFLUENCE

N REAL ESTATE, YOUR SPHERE OF INFLUENCE WILL TYPI-
cally be your primary source of business. Even if you are
selling a dozen properties a month, those whom you have a relationship with will be the ones to ask you to sell their homes or refer you
to their friends and family.

As I have mentioned, every individual in your sphere will know
several other realtors, so you have to stand out. Over the years, I
have noticed that ninety-nine percent of the time, whichever realtor
is closer to them or better friends with them is the one they hire. It
seldom comes down to experience or quality. I think it is a combination of most individuals assuming that if you have a real estate

license, you must know what you are doing. I think, even more than that, people feel guilty if they do not hire you as their agent and fear that if they don't, it will damage the relationship. Trust plays a big part in this as well. Usually, friends trust their friends, and if that friend has a real estate license, you get the picture.

I have always said that I will never let business ruin a friendship, for example, if a close friend chooses another realtor over me. I have never lost a friendship over it, but it has come close. One of my best friends used me for a year to show him properties, only to purchase a vacant lot through another realtor. The listing agent on the property told my friend that if he cut me out of the deal, the seller would knock off $30K from the price of the lot. This would have been my commission, of course.

I had another very good friend use the property manager of a multi-family property that I not only said I would list and sell for him but would also be interested in buying. The next time we saw each other, I inquired about it, and he informed me they had the property manager sell it.

Another friend had me show him property for six months, only to call me one day and inform me at the same time he was out looking with me; he was using another realtor located on the coast to show him property there as well. Can you guess where he ended up buying? He said he would mail me a gift card for all my time showing him properties. That was three years ago, and I'm still waiting for the gift card.

The point is shit happens, and even your friends will do shady things or, let's say, things they feel are in their best interest, even if it's at your expense. Keep increasing your database, and never let these deals haunt you. Focus on the future and learn from the past.

To wrap it up, your sphere of influence is the primary group you need to touch. Remember, touching does not mean physically going out and touching them, or you will wind up in big trouble. By touching, I am referring to building relationships and trying to strengthen those relationships. It is important to note once again that this must be done consistently. I promise you that if you are not consistent, another friend with a real estate license will be the one selling your friend's house. This has happened to me countless times. The more your sphere grows, the more difficult it is to maintain those relationships. Setting up systems to keep in touch will be of vital importance.

59

OPEN HOUSES

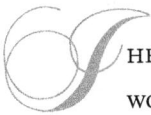

I HEAR AGENTS ALWAYS ASK THIS: "DO OPEN HOUSES work?" That is a vague question, as the answer is yes and no. In the age before the internet and websites like Realtor.com and Zillow, people shopping for homes would jump in the car on Saturday and Sunday and drive through neighborhoods looking for "Open House" signs. This would usually be their first look at the house because there were no photos online. If the buyers wanted the house, the listing agent would be thrilled as they would collect both sides of the commission—that is, if the buyers were not already working with an agent.

However, since we now live in the internet age, ninety-nine percent of home buyers begin their search online. Sites like Realtor. com and Zillow have enough information about a house to let buyers know whether they can save or eliminate that house from their search. Very few, if any, buyers walk into an open house and decide to buy. They have certainly seen the house online before their visit in most cases.

So do open houses sell homes? My answer to that is no. Now some might argue with that—sometimes an agent says, "Oh yes, my open house brought the buyer who ended up purchasing the house." I can confidently say that the buyer saw the house first online. So do open houses provide any benefit? They do, and for two reasons. The first reason is what I consider an intangible value, meaning holding open houses allows you to take photos at the home. That is an excellent opportunity for advertising on social media.

The second benefit of holding open houses is that it allows you to capture contacts for your database. Always bring a sign-in sheet and ask visitors to sign in. It can feel uncomfortable, and some might decline but always give it a try. It is important to note that just about every seller thinks open houses are something to do. Even if you tell them 99.9% of buyers search online and have their own agent, and if they want to see the property, they will call their agent and schedule a showing—sellers still have a thing for open houses.

I even had a seller join me at the open houses I held for his home. We both sat there, staring at each other for three hours, while a whopping four people came through. Because of that, you should include in your listing presentation that you will hold open houses. I always add that I try my best to monitor when people come in to look at the house, but it is difficult when you have multiple groups simultaneously. I cannot guarantee that all of your personal items are safe (or something to that effect). That is not me attempting to be deceitful or talk people out of open houses, as it is true. There have been numerous times when smaller personal items belonging to the seller disappear during open houses.

So I'll ask the question again. Do open houses work? I suppose the real answer is yes and no. They work because they allow you to generate leads, impress your seller, and post pictures on social media. But does anyone today accidentally find an open house and walk in and buy it? I'll leave it up to you to decide if spending four hours on your Sunday sitting at an open house is the way to go.

60

YOUR CIRCLE MATTERS

HAD AN AGENT ONCE WHO DID A THIRD OF THE NUMBER of deals I did one year but only made $10K less than I did. Did it frustrate me? Sure it did. Mathematically speaking, I did 66% more business than she did, yet I only made 10% more money.

Why? It was the circle she ran in. Her sphere of influence comprised individuals with a higher net worth than the circle of individuals I knew or who made up my sphere of influence. When studying the art of business, you will consistently hear mentors, authors, and other successful individuals say that you are the sum of the five closest people you hang out with. This is about your level of success. It is saying that if you want to be successful, hang out with people who are more successful than you. The same applies to the world of real estate. You need to establish and maintain relationships with individuals with higher net worth to earn more dollars per transaction.

Another agent I knew ran in such circles, and she really did not have to work as her husband made good money. She only did two to three deals one year, but one deal was a multi-million dollar property that earned her a $60K commission check. Now, if you make $250K a year, this might not impress you very much, but since the national average income of a real estate agent is $82K as of this writing, that should be impressive. Not to mention that the national average is somewhat distorted, as "most" real estate agents make about half of that amount annually.

61

FUNNY STORIES

*M*OST AGENTS HAVE EXPERIENCED FUNNY MOMENTS throughout their careers. I've had several that I'll share with you. I've also included a few stories from fellow agents who have graciously allowed me to share.

- The first house I ever sold belonged to my son's kindergarten teacher. It was my first listing, and needless to say, I was nervous about my presentation even though they assured me I had the job. The owners of the house had a rather large dog that, let's say, was more than excited that I was visiting that evening. The dog undergoing behavior training with a squirt bottle would continuously sneak under the table and shove his nose directly into my crotch. If that were not enough, he would put his paws on my legs and try to reach up and lick my face. Let me remind you—I'm trying to go through my listing presentation at the time. As the dog continued to strive for my affection, the owners would continuously squirt the dog in the face with water. While I appreciated the attempt to make the dog stop doing what it was doing, the water kept hitting me in the face. I did get the listing, but I walked out of that house soaking wet and covered in dog hair.

- Another comical moment in my career was while working with buyers showing them a house. The house was owner-occupied, but no one was supposed to be home. As we walked upstairs, we heard a commotion in one of the bathrooms, which caused me to yell out, "Realtor!" At that moment, a high school-aged boy walked out of the bathroom and then quickly shut the bathroom door and informed us we would not be permitted to go there. After a few more minutes of conversation, his girlfriend walked out of the bathroom and did the walk of shame down the stairs and out the front door. I guess his parents didn't inform him that we would be stopping by. But then again, his parents didn't think he would skip school and bring his girlfriend home.

- During another buyer showing, when no one was supposed to be home, the homeowner walked out of the bedroom in his underwear, singing at the top of his lungs. You can only imagine his surprise when he walked out and saw us standing in the middle of his living room.

- During another listing presentation, I had what I consider my shining moment in my real estate career. The owner had a dog that wanted to play fetch with me so badly. So the entire time I did my presentation, I played fetch with her Goldendoodle. Anything to get the listing, right?

- While walking in the backyard with buyers, I stepped on a massive pile of dog poop. I had to spend about 5 minutes using the hose and a small stick on the side of the house to clean it off my shoe. That really stunk! Get it?

- I had a listing early in my career where the wife refused to leave the house on the day of closing. It was their first house; needless to say; she was attached. She was so attached that she attached herself inside the closet and would not come out. My two kids were small at the time, and I vividly remember standing in the Publix parking lot trying to corral my kids, keep them from running in front of a car, and communicate with the wife through the husband. After an hour, she ended up coming out of the closet.

- I don't know if this falls into the funny category (except in how I tell it in real life), but it is interesting nonetheless. While showing a vacant home to a buyer several years ago, we were roaming around the backyard and discovered what appeared to be an urn on a bistro table on a deck near a shed. And it was occupied! Apparently, the last owners left it behind. I researched public records and discerned who he was (ironically, he was a Real Estate Mediator). He passed earlier in the year due to natural causes. I found where his widow was now living. I contacted the listing agent, and they were able to return him safely to his wife. I can just imagine the car ride after the family left the house, "Did you get Grandpa?" "No, I thought you got him!"

- I was showing a house in Saint Cloud. We walked into the master bedroom, and behind the door was a huge wax figure of Bela Lugosi as Dracula on a pedestal. The thing was like 7" tall. I got startled and jumped back and fell into my buyer, who fell back onto her husband. We went down like dominoes. When I had to send feedback, I said, "You might want to mention the vampire behind the bedroom door."

- While outside, after a showing, the buyers and I discussed the house. A wasp came out from the overhang and stung me on the lip. My lip swelled to 3 times the size in 30 seconds, and I had to drive to the nearest place for ice. Haha. I carry wasp spray now and always look for them.

- While showing a townhome, I was told the home was vacant, but when we walked up, I thought I heard a TV. I knocked and rang the doorbell several times. I unlocked the door and walked in, saying, "Hello" loudly. The tv was on, so we both jumped back outside, and I rang the doorbell again. I went back inside, thinking they must have accidentally left the TV on, and I said, "Oh, we're here to see the home, so we'll go outside and give you a few minutes." Just then, a naked girl started to get up off the couch. We jumped outside and waited for the girl and her friend to get their clothes on.

- Another of my favorites involved an attic, a loaded gun, and binoculars. Needless to say, it got weirder from there.

- This next funny story may go down as one of my favorite experiences since I've been in the real estate business. I was working with an elderly couple to list their property. The husband was a fellow guitar player, had an affinity for music, and recently purchased a microphone with a built-in amplifier. I had been out to the house on two occasions, so this was my third time, and we all felt comfortable around each other. The husband pulled out his laptop and showed me that if you type in the name of a song and "karaoke" on YouTube, a video will pop up with the music and lyrics in true karaoke fashion. He then proceeded to sing karaoke to a few of his favorite tunes, and the entire time, I was praying he wouldn't pass me the microphone. Well, he handed me the microphone and asked me what song I wanted to sing. I couldn't say no, right? I immediately started to panic and thought to myself—what song have I listened to the most over the years, and is the easiest to sing? I have no idea how I came up with "Sweet Child O' Mine" by Guns N' Roses, but that's what I picked. Slash is my favorite guitarist, but I wasn't playing guitar; I was singing! So I sang, and sang, and sang some more. I even followed that up with "Mama, I'm Coming Home" by Ozzy Osborne. Once again, something I thought I could sing. So there I was, belting out karaoke tunes on the front porch of their home. I didn't mention that, did I? They had a screened-in sunroom in the front, and that's where I was singing, right where the neighbors and anyone else who happened to walk by could hear. But I tell you what—I had one hell of a time and enjoyed it. I could have sat there all day and sung to my favorite 1980s glam rock tunes. I would have eventually had to have consumed a couple of beers to help get over just how bad I sounded, but it was one great memory!

- This scenario recently happened to me, proving that funny things still happen even after being in the business for so long. Some of you might put this story in the "dumb-dumb" category, and I am okay with that. I arrived at a house for an inspection. I was sitting in my car directly in front of the house when the inspector pulled up. I have known this inspector for years, and we have become friends, so when he pulled up, I got out of the car and walked over to him. We immediately struck up a conversation. After a few minutes of catching up, we walked up to the front door and knocked for what seemed like ten minutes. A dog was barking, and the owner opened the front door. Lo and behold, it was not my buyer. It was some guy I had never met. After an awkward few seconds, I realized I was knocking on the wrong door. I was so engaged in chatting with the inspector that I walked up to the wrong house.

62

HAVE A HOBBY (OR TWO)

*L*ET'S BE HONEST: THE REAL ESTATE BUSINESS CAN DRIVE you insane. As you should know by now, you are a business owner running a business. Whether you are doing so by yourself or with hundreds of employees, so much stress accompanies your day-to-day operations. Having a hobby or two that you enjoy is a must. It shouldn't be a choice but a mandatory part of your day or weekend, and I'm not talking about summer and winter vacations. I'm talking about things like playing the guitar for thirty minutes each day or working out every morning. These are two of my hobbies; my blood pressure would be sky-high without them!

63

WARM AND FUZZIES

YOU CAN DO MANY THINGS TO GIVE PAST AND CURRENT clients what I call "warm and fuzzies." Honestly, I completely suck in this department. Maybe because I'd rather bathe in sub-zero water than do a lot of the things I see other agents do, but, and I stress that, they do work.

Here's an example of a "warm and fuzzy" I saw recently. It is currently December and the holiday season. A local listing agent tied a big red bow around her "For Sale" sign. First, I would never think of tying a big red bow around a "For Sale" sign; second, the thought of having to shop for the big red bow makes my stomach churn. However, little things like this do make a difference. It is an intangible gesture that is hard to place a dollar amount on but helps in the grand scheme of things. Does it help sell that house faster?

Probably not, but it does make that agent look cool and gives the impression that she goes that extra mile for her clients.

Another example would be giving closing gifts. Once again, I admit my closing gifts are more practical than exciting or clever. Some would call them downright boring but look; I am not a shopper. I usually give a plain ole gift card to Lowe's or Home Depot. As I said, practical. Many agents give killer closing gifts that blow my gift card out of the water. The issue with my gift card is that it shows little effort or thought.

I recently received a gift basket from one of the mortgage brokers I use. I had just closed on another investment property and used this company. Like my boring gift card self, I am usually not impressed, nor do I get excited about a gift basket, regardless of what is inside. However, this gift basket was fantastic. It had chocolates and bottles of oil with seasonings to make a dip for bread. It was awesome, and I loved it. This same company also sent me a card for the holidays. I knew it was from them and was just about to throw it away, but I decided to open it up. Glad I did, as there was a lottery ticket inside. Most companies (real estate agents included) travel down the boring path. They will give the gift card or send the typical holiday card. But this company stands out well above the crowd by taking a little more time and effort and putting more thought into things.

64

DON'T JUST SAY NO

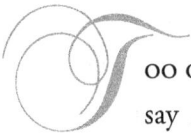

OO OFTEN, AS REAL ESTATE AGENTS, WE ARE QUICK TO say no when someone asks if we handle something outside our designated specialty. For example, an agent who only handles residential transactions is approached by someone who questions whether or not they handle commercial properties. Most of the time, that agent will quickly respond with no and say they do not but can refer them to an agent who does. In this day and age of everyone and their brother having a real estate license, you are not only losing money, but you are also losing a potential income stream that you could add to your business.

What I mean is this: Let us say you refer that commercial deal to another agent who bills themselves as a "commercial agent." The property sells for $600K, and the commission is 3%. You would have made $18,000, but instead, you referred it to another agent and made a $4,500 referral fee. Many agents who are busy and in that 20% of agents who do well and sell 80% of the real estate would be just fine with this, but if you fall into that 80% category of agents who are struggling, maybe you should not be so quick to refer that property. I would argue that even if you are an agent in that top 20%, you need to sit back and think about it before just handing that deal and client off. When you hand that client off, you are not only losing money, but you are also potentially losing another revenue stream. That one deal could turn into several, just like it might if it was a residential deal.

Now, most of you are thinking—I referred it because I know nothing about commercial real estate. It is scary and out of my area of expertise. Remember, residential real estate was intimidating and out of your area of expertise when you first entered the business. Just as you did with residential, you would be surprised what you can do when confronted with a challenge. If you seize the opportunity and get stuck, there is always someone to call if you need help. You would be amazed that the internet can help get you out of a jam in no time. Here is a quote from my new favorite motivational speaker Ed Mylett, "Champions are born by DIVING IN and ADAPTING to their circumstances." Ed goes on with more to that quote, but this first part just resonated with me, and I read it the same day I was working on this section! If you do not know who Ed is, look him up. Great speaker!

65

ADD SOME VALUE, PLEASE

*L*ET ME SHARE A STORY ABOUT TWO AGENTS THAT I hired. They were a husband and wife team, and I was genuinely excited about having them on board. The husband had just lost his job, and during our initial conversations, they suggested we partner. Without going into too much boring detail, this partnership was more like a joint venture where we targeted a specific niche. A capital investment was required, and of course, the investment of my time and focus.

About a month after we launched this joint venture, the husband informed me that he found a new job in the same industry (not real estate) he was in before but with a different company. I was happy for him as I knew it would take a while before they started making decent money in real estate, and they needed money sooner than later. The wife agreed to continue working with me on our joint venture. Fast forward a few months, I received a call where the husband informed me that the wife was going to work for another brokerage where she had a "better opportunity." Talk about an "SMH" moment. That means "shake my head" for all of you people my age or older. It took me a while to figure that one out.

Fast forward about two more years, and the husband called me one day asking if he could hang his license with me again. Being the sucker I am, I said, "Sure." The wife was still working for another brokerage, which was fine, as I did not care. The wife even proceeded to open up her own brokerage, and a few months later, guess what? You can recognize the pattern here and figure out what happened next. The husband texted me and said, "After much deliberation, I've decided to leave your brokerage and join my wife." My reply was, "I figured that was going to happen." He then proceeded to tell me how difficult of a decision it was.

We have a few things going on here and which to learn from. Aside from the obvious—I should have just said no and not been such an easy target. The agents in this story clearly had a plan and used me to get there. In fact, as of this writing, the wife, who is now a broker, continues to ask me questions on how to handle certain transactions. My advice in this situation is, first and foremost, do not use other people in a disingenuous way to get where you want to be. Secondly, make sure that if you are going to use someone, provide some value for them. Perhaps send them something from Omaha Steaks. I mean, damn, or how about just a simple thank you?

66

NEW CONSTRUCTION

CANNOT TELL YOU HOW MANY DEALS I'VE LOST TO WHAT I call the "New Construction Black Hole." It's as if new construction communities only exist to swallow up my buyers one after the other. Maybe I did not do a good enough job letting them know I could represent them, or they didn't see the value in my services. Over the years, I have had buyer after buyer walk into a new construction sales office and sign a contract, which cut me entirely out of the deal.

Make sure your sphere of influence knows you can represent them with new construction purchases and why you can add value. Please do not rely on the sales reps at the new construction office to do you any favors whatsoever, as it is my opinion that the vast majority do not want a buyer's agent present. Remember that the sales office agent is working for the builder; your buyer needs to know that.

Also, give potential buyers your business card or go with them when they first walk into that office. Many builders have a policy that if you are not present with your buyer when you first walk in, you are not entitled to a commission. BS if you ask me, but that is the deal. Other builders will only give you your commission if you are present when the contract is signed. I had that situation happen to me. I had been showing new construction property to my buyer for weeks and even was present when we toured the community in which they ended up buying. However, I was out of town when they signed the contract, and the builder's policy was that if the agent was not there, that agent was not entitled to a commission. Once again, a BS move on the builder's part, and I probably had a procuring cause case, but I chose not to get entangled with attorneys to pursue it. So the moral of the story is to make sure everyone you know realizes they are better off being represented by you when searching for new construction homes.

Make sure you actually add some value and do not just sit along for the ride while the sales rep and builder do all the work, as your buyer will notice that. If you have little experience with new construction builds, grab a cup of coffee and start searching online (or ask your mentor) how you can help buyers with new construction purchases. Even if it seems trivial or unimportant, try and look like you are engaged and not just counting the days until you receive your check. I have even fallen victim to the hypnotic tone of the sales rep spearheading things while I sit back and calculate my commission check on my smartphone.

67

PUT IN THE HOURS

OTAL HOW MANY HOURS YOU *ACTUALLY* WORK DURING the week, not the amount of time you think you are working just because you have your phone turned on. Too many agents think they work full-time and end up wasting a lot of time. Successful individuals use a calendar, not a list. Many realtors do not use either, unfortunately. Try and schedule your day into blocks of time. There are all sorts of books out there that can help you. Some are real estate-specific, and others are more general. If I had to choose, my favorite two for helping me to improve the way I schedule my day are "Atomic Habits" and "The 4 Disciplines of Execution."

68

DON'T GET TOO BIG
FOR YOUR BRITCHES

OW MY GRANDMA USED THAT EXPRESSION, SO IT'S A
pretty old one. That means do not get too full of yourself or get a fat head thinking you are the shit. As an investor, I have
made several calls to agents in other markets. I have done that all my
career, and I'm sure many of you have, too—referring clients who
are moving to other cities.

After I had started my real estate fund, I asked a friend in a particular market I was looking into if she had a trusted agent whom she
could refer. I did not know at the time whether this agent had any
experience with investing or his qualifications, and I did not provide
my friend with any details other than I was looking for investment

property in that area. She contacted her friend, and her friend responded that he or someone on his team would be happy to help her. Perhaps I'm being sensitive, but that rubbed me the wrong way. I am guessing this agent figured I was just another "guy" looking to buy a house in his market. I assume he is a "top producer" and has his team with a buyer's agent, so he figured he would pass me off to his buyer's agent as usual. Unfortunately, it rubbed me so badly that I threw his name in the trash. Little did he know, he lost out on, let us say, a lot of money coming through his pipeline for perhaps several years down the road.

My point is this—if someone refers someone to you, make the call or speak to that person directly before deciding how to best handle that potential client. You never know when that "big dog" might be calling!

69

HAVE AN
ACCOUNTABILITY
PARTNER

ONLY REALIZED THE IMPORTANCE OF HAVING AN AC-
countability partner once I started going to the gym
with my buddy Sean. I had heard about the benefits of having an
accountability partner for years and read it in numerous sections
in books, but I felt uncomfortable seeking one out. There was
also the aspect that I did not want to add another person to the
list for whom I needed to be accountable as the list was already
long. Honestly, I wasn't even thrilled about suddenly having a
workout partner, as I always worked out alone with headphones.
No talking and just blasting my favorite playlist was my gig. But

I soon realized that having Sean as my workout partner did two things.

First, many of those mornings when I would find an excuse not to go to the gym stopped, as I knew I had to meet Sean. The feeling of not letting him down and even the thought of him thinking I was being lazy was enough to get me there.

Secondly, it forced me to try new exercises. I had created such a habit of spending too much time in the gym repeatedly doing the same thing. I was getting bored, and it is good to mix up your workouts. So not only did I start doing different exercises, but I also learned about new ones. Then BAM! Suddenly, it hit, and I thought, "Damn, an accountability partner works." So what did I immediately do next? Yep, another obvious one here—I went and found myself a real estate accountability partner. I cannot express in words the difference it made in my business.

70

DON'T CASH THAT CHECK BEFORE THE DEAL CLOSES

OO OFTEN, WE SECURE A LISTING OR BUYER AND PUNCH the projected sale amount multiplied by the commission percentage in the calculator. At least, I know I do, as I like to see what I will make on the deal. It is something you should do, as it should play a part in helping you decide whether you want to take the deal. If you spend six months driving time-sucking buyers around for a $2,000 commission, you might think twice before taking the deal.

However, it is important to realize that whether the potential commission is $2,000 or $20,000, that money is not guaranteed. Do not spend it, do not worry about it, and do not take your family on a Mediterranean cruise trip and put it on your credit card, thinking you will pay it off when that commission check comes in. As I write this section, I have just lost approximately $50K in commission from deals falling through. I'm sure many of you just threw up in your mouth after reading that. Yes, it makes me sick to my stomach too, but the longer you are in this business, you will realize that this is just part of it. Not all deals will work out. Of course, losing the big commission deals is harder to swallow than the deals where you would make a modest amount. Just realize that is part of the business; press on, and do not look in the rear-view mirror.

71

LEAD GENERATION

F I WERE PUTTING CHAPTERS IN ORDER OF IMPORTANCE, I'd have this one at the top or close to it. You have to spend time generating leads and increasing your sphere of influence. Once again, let me reiterate, YOU MUST SPEND TIME GENERATING LEADS AND INCREASING YOUR SPHERE OF INFLUENCE, regardless of how you do it.

You don't have to use an expensive CRM. I started with a CRM but was not too fond of it and switched to using an EXCEL spreadsheet. Now I'm back to a CRM as I found one I like to use. TOMA comes into play here, too. Emails, phone calls, texts, social media posts, happy hour, dinners, morning coffee—anything you can do to stay in front of people and let them know you are the resident real estate expert. But the critical point is you must keep increasing the number of people in your sphere.

72

BUY AN ELECTRONIC LOCKBOX, YOU CHEAPSKATE!

T THE TIME OF THIS WRITING, AN ELECTRONIC LOCKBOX costs $150. Apparently, that is a high price for many agents as they continue to use their antiquated combination boxes. Don't get me wrong; there is a time and a place for using a combination box. I use them frequently when rehabbing a property and needing to grant my contractors access. But today, why would you continue to use a cheap and old combination box instead of the super high-tech ole ELB?

The primary reason I can think of is that the agent is cheap and doesn't want to spend the money. Now, the problem I have with agents continuing to use these combination boxes is obvious if you have ever tried opening one. Some are like tiny Rubik's Cubes where you can't figure out how they open after entering the combination.

The second reason I can't stand these boxes is something I just encountered after eighteen years in the industry. I was scheduling a showing to see a condo in Orlando. The property was vacant. Okay, fine, here we go. After entering the requested time, I received an immediate email indicating that my showing requests were approved. However, as I usually received the code for the combination, this time was different. The instructions indicated that I would be notified of the code at the time of the showing and only through the Showing Time app. Well, I don't have the fricken Showing Time app, nor do I have time to figure out how to download it. But I did try, and in all honesty, I did give it about ten minutes before I gave up and called the listing agent and said, "Just give me the damn code!"

I almost went as far as saying, "If you weren't a cheapskate and bought an electronic lockbox, you would not have to inconvenience everyone who wants to show your property." For all I know, everyone reading this has the Showing Time app.

73

MINDSET

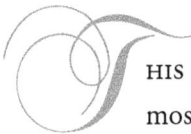

HIS IS PERHAPS—NOT PERHAPS, IT IS—THE SINGLE most important concept for you to grasp in this entire book. You have to have the right mindset to be successful in this business. So what does that mean? I'll keep it as simple as I had heard it before. The thoughts you have today are where you will end up tomorrow, in five years, ten years, and twenty years. What you watch, what you read, and the friends you associate yourself with help you paint the narrative of what will become "you."

So if you want to be successful, whether in the real estate business or all areas of your life, then "train." Listen to successful people on a podcast or YouTube, read their books, and follow them on Instagram. You will be amazed that the more quality you consume, your taste for brain-goo content like reality TV, Netflix, and even the news will become nonexistent. You will only come to crave more and more quality content—content that will help you improve in all areas of your life.

74

NEVER DIVULGE YOUR SELLER'S BOTTOM LINE

JUST EXPERIENCED THIS ONE FOR THE FIRST TIME, AND fortunately, it was right before I sent this off for publishing. I had the time to include it in the book, as you, like me, will be flabbergasted when you read the story.

I was purchasing a property for my real estate fund and found a condo in Orlando I liked. It was listed at $140K and had an existing tenant. My initial offer was $120K, and I was prepared to get the deal done as high as $135K. When I submitted my offer, the listing agent immediately responded, "My seller won't do that, but he will take $125K as that is his bottom line." I would if I could insert the hit myself in the face emoji here. Needless to say, I said "done deal" and sent my revised offer within five minutes. I could not believe she basically robbed her seller of $10K. Never let your seller's bottom line be known!

75

"LOCK IT DOWN"

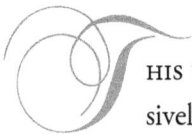

HIS USED TO BE A PHRASE USED PRETTY MUCH EXCLU-sively by real estate investors. It refers to the tactic or process when a property is identified as a potential investment opportunity; the investor submits an offer before seeing the property in person to "lock it down." They get the property under contract as soon as possible before someone else has a chance to submit an offer and then decide during the inspection period whether to proceed with the purchase. It is a common practice today due to a shortage of inventory levels with primary occupant buyers. The result is many listing agents are now requiring that the buyer must see the property in person first before submitting an offer.

76

YOU ARE WHAT YOU EAT

"YOU ARE WHAT YOU EAT"—EVERYONE IS FAMILIAR WITH this saying, yet most Americans are overweight or feel sluggish all day due to a poor diet. As I have mentioned before, I have always struggled with my diet. I am on the road so much that my choices are to pack a cooler with healthy foods, which takes a lot of preparation and effort or shoot through the McDonald's drive-through for that two-cheeseburger meal. Tough call, especially when those tasty burgers have 30 grams of protein between the two, and I need that protein for lifting weights, right?

See how easily that can be justified? Just like "you are what you eat," you are what you consume. I am not referring to consuming food but the things you consume through your eyes and ears. Do you spend all morning and night watching Netflix or consuming educational content? Yeah, I'll admit I did learn a lot about history watching "The Last Kingdom" on Netflix, which was fantastic, but it is not the same, trust me. If you don't like to read, podcasts are great, and YouTube is also excellent for podcasts, interviews, and more. Try your best to eat healthy, exercise, and consume educational content. Your daily performance levels will increase dramatically.

77

CONCLUSION

*I*T TOOK FOUR YEARS TO FINISH THIS BOOK. IT WASN'T until last year that I included it on my calendar and decided to work on it every day for 30 minutes as soon as I got to the office. That quickly became a habit, and the next thing I knew, I had the book ready to hand over to the editor.

Everyone's journey in life is different, and everyone has unique obstacles to overcome. However, you will be unstoppable if you do a few things right every day.

Hopefully, you enjoyed the book, and if you picked up even a single tip that will help you on your journey, that's a win. Like many of you, I used to be a non-reader, and sitting down to read was a challenge. I read page after page, and when I finished, I had no recollection of what I had just consumed. Another goal of mine was to make this book an easy read. Hopefully, it was even a bit entertaining. So to all of you other real estate professionals, keep grinding daily and remember success is not a straight path but a journey of what can seem like traveling through an impenetrable force field at times. However, if you stay the course, you shall prevail in the end.

And that's a wrap!

SUGGESTED READING LIST

Rich Dad Poor Dad by Robert T. Kiyosaki

The Millionaire Real Estate Agent by Gary Keller

The Millionaire Real Estate Investor by Gary Keller

Extreme Ownership by Jocko Willink

Can't Hurt Me by David Goggins

The Cashflow Quadrant by Robert T. Kiyosaki

Stillness is Key by Cal Newport

Shut up and Listen! by Tilman Fertitta

The Parasitic Mind by Gad Saad

SOLD: Every Real Estate Agent's Guide to Building a Profitable Business by David Greene

The Power of One More by Ed Mylett

Think Straight by Darius Foroux

Never Split the Difference by Chris Voss with Tahl Raz

War of Art: Break Through the Blocks and Win Your Inner Creative Battles by Steven Pressfield and Shawn Coyne

The One Thing by Jay Papasan and Gary Keller

Deep Work by Cal Newport

The Midas Touch by Donald J. Trump and Robert T. Kiyosaki

The 10x Rule by Grant Cardone

Big Money Energy by Ryan Serhant

Winning by Tim S. Grover

Psychology of Money by Morgan Housel

Compound Effect by Darren Hardy

Mindset by Carol S. Dweck, Ph.D.

The Obstacle Is the Way by Ryan Holiday

Fit for Success by Nick Shaw

Vivid Vision by Cameron Herold

Tax-Free Wealth by Tom Wheelwright, CPA

Younger Next Year by Chris Crowley and Henry S. Lodge, MD with Allan J. Hamilton, MD

Who Not How by Dan Sullivan with Dr. Benjamin Hardy

Think Like a Monk by Jay Shetty

The 4 Disciplines of Execution by Chris McChesney, Steven Covey, and Jim Huling

How to Win Friends and Influence People by Dale Carnegie

The Subtle Art of Not Giving a F*ck by Mark Manson

Breath by James Nestor

The 4-Hour Workweek by Tim Ferris

Think and Grow Rich by Napoleon Hill

ABOUT THE AUTHOR

A native Floridian his entire life, originally from Miami, FL, and a graduate of the University of Florida, Pat now lives in Orlando, FL, and has been in the real estate business since 2004. He has served in various capacities, such as the Broker and Owner of his real estate brokerage, The Thomas Lynne Realty Group, and a Managing Partner of the real estate investment firm Southern Mountain

Capital. His favorite pastime is spending time with his wife Angie and children Zach and Emily. As a native Floridian, it's not surprising that his favorite vacation destination remains to this day: the beach or on a boat.

OFFICE: Thomas Lynne Capital, LLC
7380 W Sand Lake Road, Suite 500
Orlando, FL 32819

PHONE: 407.808.0899

EMAIL: Patrick@thomaslynnecapital.com

WHAT PATRICK'S CLIENTS ARE SAYING

"When it comes to finding a true professional that gets the job done – look no further than Pat Hancock! There are a ton of Realtors that talk a good game, but Pat makes it happen! His caring attitude, knowledge, dedication, commitment, and hard work are just a few things that set him apart when making your buying & selling decisions."

- Rhett Kilmer, Buyer/Seller

"Patrick is a true professional to work with. He genuinely seems to have the client's best interest when it comes to selling RE. His knowledge, expertise, and people he has in place makes each transaction a pleasant experience."

- Tracy Canning, Realtor and Mentor

"Very professional and easy to work with. Made my long-distance purchase of a house easy. Not only did I buy my house with him, but he is now managing the property. Rented my property within 8 hours of listing it. Trustworthy and knowledgeable. Would recommend highly."

- Rochelle, Real Estate Investor